Mary Hayes
(901) 895-1073

Stenciled Quilts for Christmas

by
Marie Monteith Sturmer

AQS American Quilter's Society
P. O. Box 3290 • Paducah, KY 42002-3290

To my dear children,
son Jim,
daughter-in-law Joan and
grandson Carl.

Additional copies of this book may be ordered from:

American Quilter's Society
P.O. Box 3290
Paducah, KY 42002-3290

@ $14.95, add $1.00 for postage and handling.

Table of Contents

Acknowledgments

This book has been a joy for me, but I could not have done it alone. I am grateful to my husband, Ralph, who worked so patiently with me in the photographing of the quilts. A special thank you goes to Ellen Allen for deciphering my scribblings on her computer, to Lois Lambert for quilting several wallhangings, and to my dear friend, Marvel Ide for her kindness in wanting to help with the hemming of some quilts. I appreciate the use of the unique willow furniture from The Twiggery Studio, made by my nephew, Clifton Monteith.

Collection of Stenciled Christmas Quilts

(B) Beginner **(I) Intermediate** **(A) Advanced**

Introduction

The collection of stenciled projects in this book is comprised of Christmas related quilts. You might ask, "Why Christmas quilts?"

Thinking back on my many years as an art teacher, I pondered the lessons I enjoyed teaching the most. The Christmas projects were without a doubt my favorites. I loved the papier maché Santa puppets, the linoleum block printed Christmas cards, the paper cutout sleighs and Rudolphs, and most of all, the stenciled neckties for Dads and stenciled scarfs and handkerchiefs for Moms. The children's response to Christmas projects was always a joy. Those were happy days for me and now, years later, the enchantment of the season is flowing over into my own Christmas quilt projects.

Each quilt in this collection has a personality of its own. Some are bold, some are delicate and fancy. Some have bright colors. A variety of designs are all carefully tied to the one theme.

As I entertained one idea, there was always another waiting to be nurtured. Imagination is a rare seedling that everyone should cultivate.

When you read through this book, may your thoughts of a stenciled quilt be visible in your mind's eye and with my assistance, may it become a reality. Then with your enthusiasm and persistence you will experience the joy of making a stenciled quilt.

Historical Sketches

The turn of the 19th century brought about many wonderful changes to the American society. Some of the early families that had migrated to America were now in their second and third generations. Prosperity was on their horizon. Their humble starter homes, crudely constructed log cabins with dirt floors and few windows, if any, were now being used by their livestock or were housing their precious farm equipment. Some log cabins at this time were converted into schoolhouses.

Nearly every thriving New England community of any size had their own logging mill where large quantities of cut lumber was produced. Post and beam construction for a home was being replaced by the framing system of stud and lath. Families were now constructing more sophisticated homes with stonewall foundations. The outside of many homes were covered over with horizontal lapped board siding. Double hung windows were used, the nine over six light was a popular style. The interior walls were plastered and the floors were constructed of wide plank boards.

You can just imagine how excited the women living in these newly built homes must have been. Their thoughts, undoubtedly, were occupied with notions of making their home more comfortable and attractive. A new wave of concern for home embellishments swept the country in the early 1800's, when women of all classes gave into the movement of the creative decorative arts.

The women who lived in the larger cities had no difficulties with their decorating projects. They had money to spend and could very well send to England for hand painted wallpapers and fine fabrics. Many of these imported wallpapers were hand stenciled on paper that resembled fine fabrics. Flocked wallpapers were made by combining powdered wool with the stencil paint, producing a fuzzy-like texture. Block printing techniques were often superimposed on a stenciled background. These sumptuous wallpapers were very costly and far beyond the means of many. The affluent were the only recipients of such luxury. Some of the chintz fabrics used for draperies and applique quilts came from as far away as India.

Many city women were in a well-to-do economic situation. Their husbands held impressive business positions with rewarding salaries, only to be found in the cities. Thus their homes could reflect all the splendor of the combined elegance of the English and European influence which was coupled with the best of American craftmanship.

However, the women who lived in remote rural areas were not so fortunate. They had little or no money to spend on frivolous home decorations, so they had to improvise. This make-do attitude brought with it an innovative spirit and made a profound mark that distinguishes American folk art from all other art trends.

In the small New England towns of Dublin and Hancock, New Hampshire, lived a very artistic, very ambitious man by the name of Moses Eaton, Jr. (1796-1886). He is known today for his creative wall stenciling that started a whole new craze of interior decorating in the mid-1800's.

Eaton was an itinerant artist who traveled the backroads of the New England countryside painting stencil designs on plaster walls of countless new homes. He certainly was the answered prayer of the rural housewife. She did not have to wait months on end for a shipment of expensive wallpaper to come from England. At the coming of the itinerant artist, she could have her home stenciled with beautiful unique designs within a week or so.

Sometimes a series of stencil designs were used to encompass an entire wall area including the expanse over a fireplace, while other times stencil border designs were employed as a frieze or as a wainscoting or at the baseboard.

Stencil designs were not used just as wall decorations, but often were used on floors. Designs were worked into overall patterns to simulate a rug, which was at that time a very scarce commodity. Border designs edging the perimeter of a room were a quick way of establishing a decorative theme.

These stenciling services by the itinerant artist were accomplished by bartering, thus the rural housewife could have her house adorned in a most original fashion in exchange for little more than providing the artist with board and room. It is thought that Moses Eaton, Jr. had many students who served an apprenticeship with him. His original designs have been found painted in homes as far south as New Jersey and as far west as central Pennsylvania, however, Eaton himself never left the New England states.

The men were acclaimed as the wall stencilers and have always had this honor attributed to them.

There has been no substantial findings to date that the women were ever known as wall stencilers. This does not mean that the women were about to be left out of the history books. The women readily began to stencil on fabric for window curtains, bed curtains, pillows and table cloths. They stenciled floors, furniture and floorcloths. Like the men stencilers, they used stencils made of stiff leather, metal or shellac-coated cardboard.

The first floorcloths were made in England. When the people in the colonies began to make their own floorcloths, the English market suffered greatly. These floorcloths were made of heavy sail canvas and were painted with lively stencil designs and sealed with many coats of varnish. The housewife found they were easy to make, long lasting and added a delightful decorator's touch.

The women, becoming stencilers in their own right, were looking for new and different ways to use stencils. For a fascinating project, they took several widths of long lengths of homespun woven fabric and sewed them together, fashioning them into a whole-cloth. These whole-cloth components were in turn stenciled with designs that often covered the entire cloth, detailing designs of flowers, birds and fruit. The whole-cloth then became a bedspread sometimes known as a counterpane. Stenciled spreads were used to cover up the old worn quilts and comforters, giving the bedroom a fresh look of instant decorating.

It was not long before the women began to make these stenciled spreads into lovely quilts. Arranging the spread (now called a quilt top) with a layer of cotton batting or a wool fleece and another whole-cloth for the back, comprised the making of a quilt. These three layers were held together in place with many rows of running stitches, called quilting stitches. These quilting stitches gave a very decorative treatment to the quilt when stitched in fancy patterns of feathers, birds, braids and scrolls.

Extraordinary things happened when the quilting took place on a stenciled spread. The stencil paint had changed the surface texture of the fabric and when the quilting stitches were held close to the stenciled design, the design would puff up and take on the characteristics of applique work and in some instances, trapunto work. Trapunto is a very decorative high relief design worked with outline stitches and is padded with extra batting from the underside of the quilt.

The overall feeling of a quilted, stenciled spread gives the illusion of an old applique quilt. A traditional applique quilt is made of many small pieces of fabric cut to a pattern and hand stitched to a background fabric. If the quilt design is complex and intricate, the technique is very time consuming and sometime takes years to complete a full-size quilt. The applique quilts before 1750 were all made of whole-cloth. Just before the Revolutionary War, many applique quilts were made of four large quilt blocks which were much easier to handle and to work on. Applique Album quilts became fashionable after the Civil War and were usually made up of smaller blocks of 12" squares. Album quilts became a pastime activity and were often referred to as the ladies "pick-up" work.

Not all women were competent when it came to quiltmaking and all the et ceteras it entails. Perhaps their interests were taken with theorem painting so popular in the mid-1800's. Theorem, meaning a method of painting using a set of rules or a formula, was first fashionable in England. Painted on velvet or velour-type fabric with oil paint or on paper with watercolor paint, the basic painting was done with a series of stencils and finished with freehand brush strokes for details. Fruit basket still life paintings were the most common subjects. It is assumed that many of the theorem painters were the first to create stenciled spreads.

The stenciled quilt just had to have been a source of inspiration for the housewife of the 1800's. Their busy days left only sparce intervals of time for needlework. Because the stenciled quilt was quick and easy to create and very attractive, it lured the attention of many a rural housewife who, by the way, was the predominant maker of the stenciled quilt. Stenciling techniques were mastered through trial and error methods by these self-sufficient women. Their stenciling ideas were as individual as their own personalities.

I am sure the women were overwhelmed with the unending possibilities of a stenciled quilt. To study some of these old quilts furnishes us with facts that relate to the tastes and preferences of the women of that time. The simplicity of some stencil designs suggest a meager lifestyle, while a more complex design, perhaps of some exotic flowers, is indicative of one enjoying abundance.

The inspiration of the stencils are a clue to the heritage of the quiltmaker. The immigrants brought remnants of their cultures to America in many unusual ways. Small items such as clothing, elaborately stitched in old traditional folk art patterns,

a charger etched with the family crest depicting fictitious animals, or illustrated manuscripts bound in an embossed leather cover. These were precious items full of revered meanings. It is no wonder we can find evidences of legendary designs taken from such treasures in what we call true American folk art.

The women who were without such sentimental resources and had not been exposed to such attitudes picked up on ideas at hand. Those who were not apt at drawing took their ideas directly from nature, such as a rose or oak leaf and worked it into their stencil design. The women, much like the men stencilers, borrowed and exchanged stencil designs. Many times this was done unbeknown to the creating artist. This, however, was all a part of the pioneer spirit of sharing. No one person claimed a corner on any one thing. It was not until people became more economically independant that they also became more possessive about things they made. It is refreshing to note that this pioneer spirit of sharing is still prevalent today among the thousands of active quilting groups throughout our land.

A stenciled quilt dating to the mid-1800's is a precious find, a priceless piece of pure American folk art. Today there are very few, perhaps thirty-five original stenciled quilts that are documented in museums across the country. Some of the outstanding museums are: The Henry Ford Museum in Dearborn, Michigan; the Old Sturbridge Village in Massachusetts; the Rockefeller Folk Art Center in Williamsburg, Virginia; the Shelburne Museum in Vermont; the Winterthur Museum in Delaware and the Museum of American Folk Art in New York City.

The stenciled quilt certainly was a good idea. Nevertheless within a short period of fifteen years (1820-1835), it turned out to be not such a good idea. As time went on the women became a little wiser when they discovered their stencil painted fabric items were not durable and so they just stopped making them.

The decline in stenciled quilts is attributed to the poor quality of paint used during this period. When the women first started to make stenciled fabric projects they used their dye water prepared for yarns and fabrics. A water soluble additive called gum arabic was used to thicken the dye water so it could be used as a stencil paint. Gum arabic was a very common product made from the Acacia tree which grows in the Southern United States. It could be obtained from the general store or from the country peddler and was sometimes used for making furniture polish and was used in cooking recipes such as Christmas candies. The concoction of dye water paint was very unsatisfactory. Even the mordants in the dye water were not effective enough in making the paint permanent. The colors either faded away, wore away or washed away with laundering.

The next attempt for making a good stencil paint was only a slightly better way. The housewife purchased dry ground powdered pigments that were intended to be used for painting barns, houses and farm implements. These dry pigments were mixed with a very thick, yellow boiled oil, known today as linseed oil. If the amounts of pigment and oil were not just right, the oil would separate from the pigment and would bleed out into the fabric when painted through the stencil opening, leaving a brownish halo line around the painted design. But with a little practice, this problem could be controlled. These oil paints were by far the best paints at this time to be used for stenciling on fabric, although there was a drawback. These paints were intended for exterior use and could withstand harsh weather conditions so they all contained large quantities of lead, iron and salt. These properties had an adverse effect on the fabric, in some cases literally eating away the fabric.

The few remaining stenciled quilts (1820-on) that are in good condition are ones that were most likely painted with artist oil paints, many of which were imported from Europe.

The poor stencil paint was the demise of the stenciled quilt era. Time however has a way of replacing all things and today we can again create beautiful stenciled quilts as our ancestors did in their clever folk art ways. The laboratory tested latex and acrylic paints of today afford us endless opportunities to produce fabric stenciled projects that will be lasting reminders and heirlooms of the 1990's.

Collection of Stenciled Christmas Quilts

Photos and Critiques

It is with pleasure
that I present my collection of
stenciled Christmas quilts.

FATHER CHRISTMAS

FATHER CHRISTMAS
28" x 28" whole-cloth quilt with stenciled design.

What a charmer this little wallhanging turned out to be! With the traditional color scheme of red and green, Father Christmas takes his stance for the holidays. Size wise, this wallhanging would fit into the smallest wall space and still become the most intriguing decoration of all. Waffle quilting stitches comfortably fill the background. The sound waves of concentric quilting ridges marked with an architect's flexible curve focus the attention around Father Christmas, while the circle of holly leaves reinforces this conformation. Arrange the holly leaf wreath stencil so the center stems form a 15½" circle. Look for this holly wreath stencil design on the Garland of Holly quilt (Page 18). The features of the face are inked in with an ballpoint laundry marker.

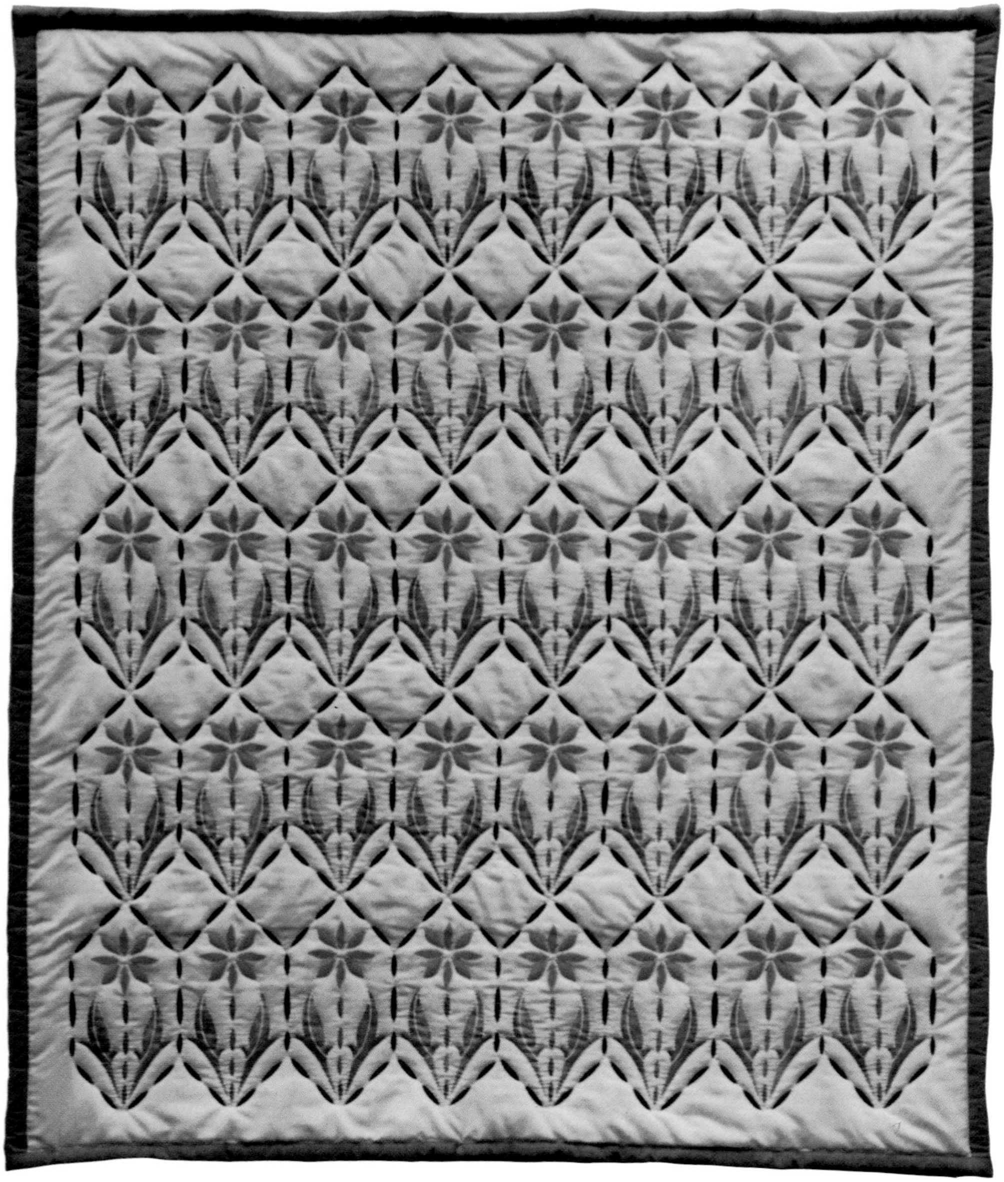

HOLIDAY FLOWER GARDEN
45" x 54½" whole-cloth quilt with stenciled design.

A very pleasant display of bright flowers being repeated over and over again in an uninterrupted simplicity is a happy expression of the gala day. The broken black interlaced hexagon lines create an arabesque style which define each complete plant, giving a regimental impression of a patchwork quilt. The wide bridges in the green leaves provide spaces for showy quilting lines. This whole-cloth quilt is easy to stencil once true horizontal and vertical lines are established. When drawing plans for this design, I knew the stationary flowers would need to be accompanied by a rhythmic accent. The flair of the leaves functions in just this way. This stencil design would adapt well to most any color scheme and would adjust to any size quilt. All stencil parts are outline quilted.

FESTIVE LILY
43½" x 43½" patchwork quilt with stenciled design.

This symmetrical floral design is my modified version of the Virginia Lily or North Carolina Lily quilt design that was popular in Pennsylvania during the 1820's. Confusion of quilt names has long been a topic of conversation as each quiltmaker always liked to add her own title. The Lily design is also known as the Tulip or Peony design. The flowers of these old designs were pieced and the stems were made of appliqued strips. By working four flower motifs into one large quilt block, I have created a center motif that forms the nucleus of the design. Sashing borders of red and green, acting as framing, set each block apart which in turn are all united by the outer light green and red borders. Outline quilting surrounds each stencil design and the sashing and borders are quilted in the ditch.

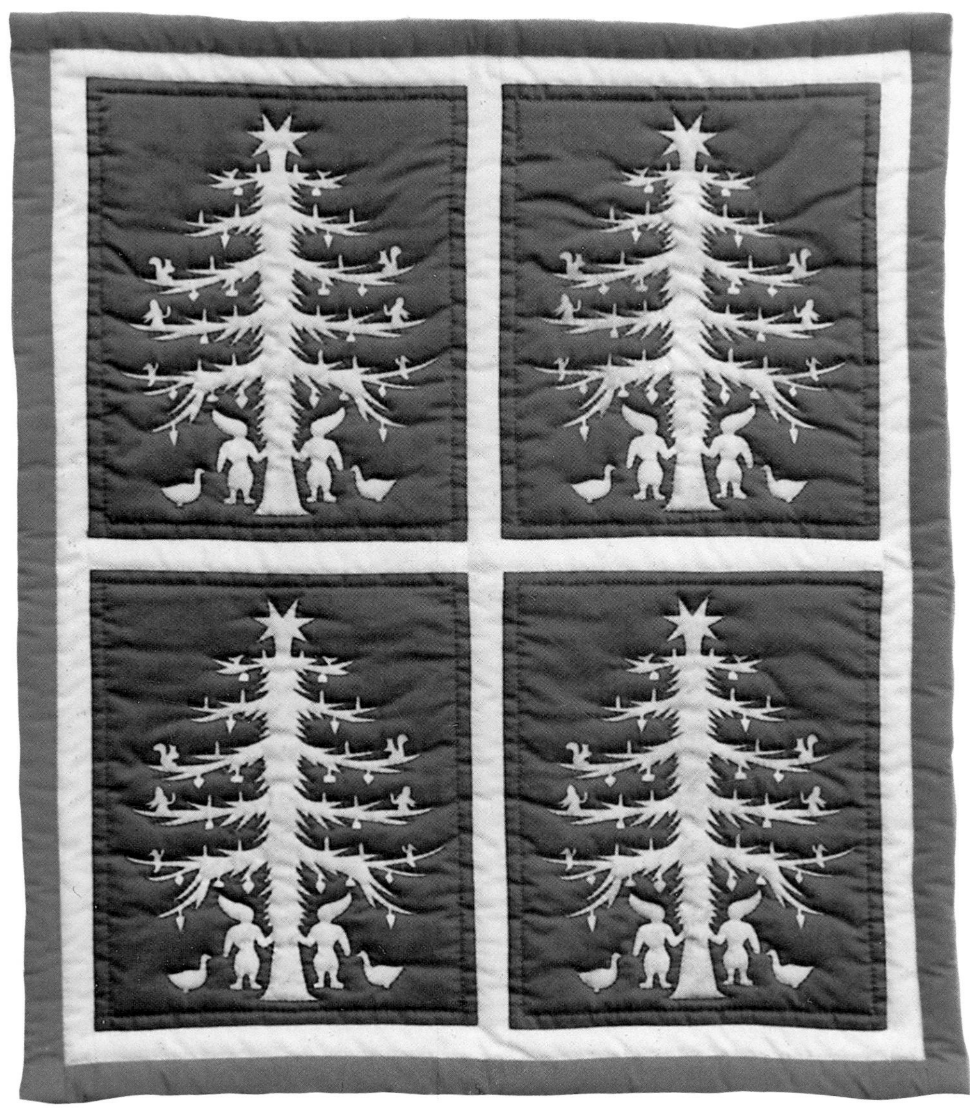

SCHERENSCHNITTE
24¾" x 29¾" patchwork quilt with stenciled design.

This original cut paper Christmas tree with elves and geese was made in 1953 and given to my son as a gift. Paper cuttings similar to this design were made by the early Pennsylvania Germans and are now prized by folk art collectors. The word "Scherenschnitte" means "scissor cutting," and is actually a word of both German and Swiss origin. This is a very interesting craft because it can be used for so many different occasions. Symmetrical designs of folded cut paper were used for wedding, baptismal and birth certificates in the 18th and 19th centuries. Valentines, book illustrations and kitchen shelf borders were popular during the Victorian period. For my quilt, I found it necessary to apply several layers of white paint on the dark fabric. I did not remove the stencil allowing the paint to dry before proceeding to paint again. The quilting was good discipline for me, a chance to work on smaller stitches that followed the very intricate parts of the design. Matching green thread was used for outline quilting around the stencil. White thread was used for quilting in the ditch for the white fabric.

DRESDEN PLATE
45" x 65" whole-cloth quilt with stenciled design. Quilted by Lois Lambert.

The Dresden Plate was a favorite scrap quilt pattern. Small pieces of fabric reclaimed from the better parts of old clothing could be used. These bits of fabric have preserved inklings of past fashions. My whole-cloth stenciled interpretation of the Dresden Plate design is totally contemporary. The printed fabric of the wedge-shaped pieces is gone, being replaced by solid reds and greens, leaving only the structured shape of the plate. The sashing, in a fluctuating arrangement of green diamonds and red dots, causes a rapid intertwining movement resembling a flashing neon sign. The dark green border restricts the bounds of such activity. The addition of the bright green cotton perle embroidery floss worked in the buttonhole stitch could be the only personalized clue relating to old Dresden Plate quilts. I stitched the floss through the three layers of the quilt creating an interesting design on the back side. The quilt is now attractive enough to be used on both sides. When working on a whole-cloth quilt such as this, the stenciling always starts in the middle and is worked out to the border edges. The stencils are outline quilted, excluding red dots, and the border is quilted in the ditch.

WEDDING RING BOUQUET
54" x 58" patchwork quilt with stenciled design.

This Bouquet design is akin, in name and piecing procedure, to the Double Wedding Ring design and became very popular in the early 1920's when the quilters found the piecing so much easier. In making my stencils, I have simplified the design and formed wide bands of white fabric by the use of stencil bridges. These bridge areas are just perfect for showing off nice even quilting stitches. I used the Mylar™ stencils for a quilting template on the red fabric, which by the way, is printed with miniature white hearts, so appropriate for a wedding quilt. I pieced the quilt top before I stenciled the designs. Be sure to cut a stencil for each shade of green. All designs were outline quilted with white thread. The white blocks were quilted in the ditch.

GARLAND OF HOLLY
48" x 57½" patchwork quilt with stenciled design.

Four long white panels and three wide green sashing strips comprise this simple quilt. The green border adds the finishing touch. The large red bows interspersed with the meandering holly greens add a festive spark. The holly stencil is the same one used for the Father Christmas wallhanging (page 12). By turning the stencil unit in different directions it adds a nice serpentine movement. Each holly leaf has a wide bridge for the center vein exposing the background fabric. The quilting lines follow both sides of the stenciled stems and only the leaf bridges. The bows are completely outline quilted and all the ditches are quilted. I prepared the quilt top before stenciling.

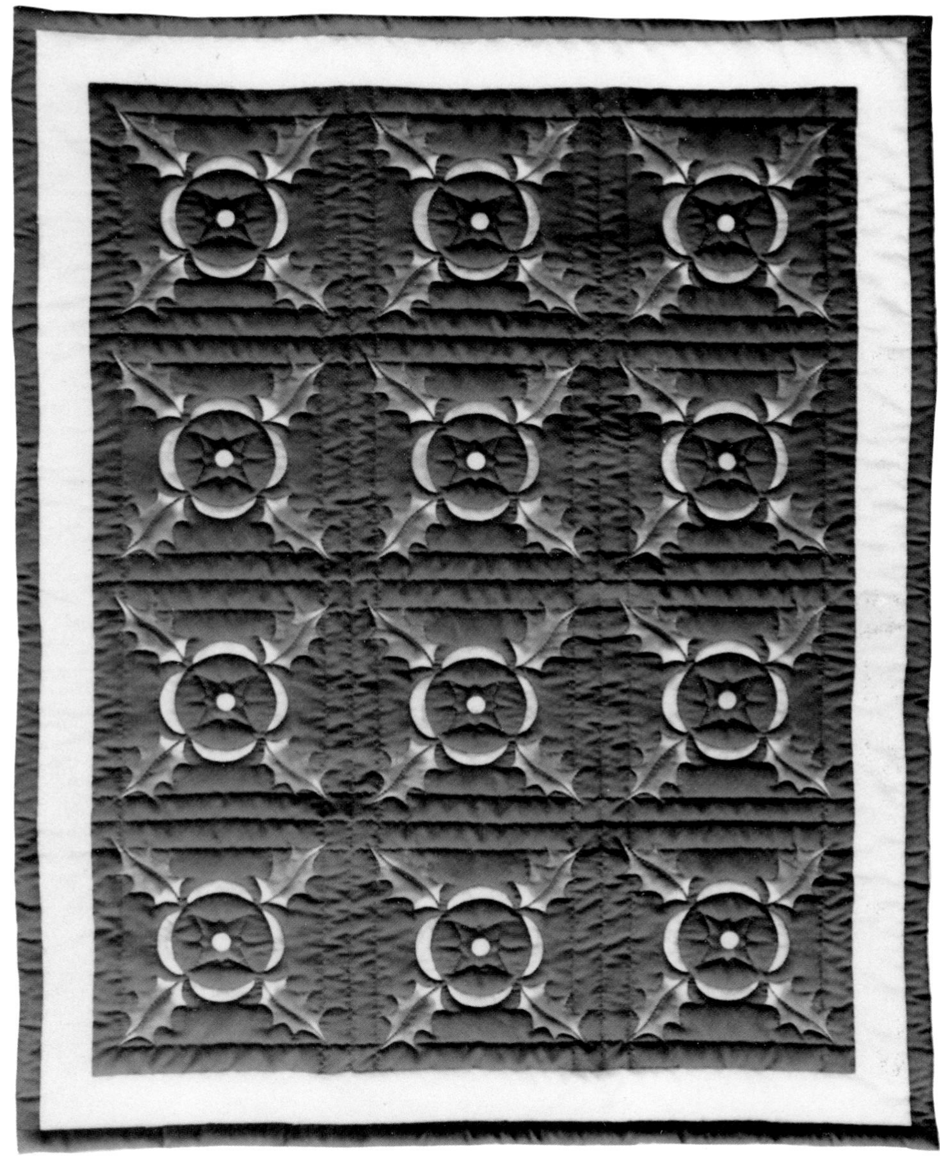

HOLLY LEAF AND REEL
41" x 51" whole-cloth quilt with pieced border and stenciled design. Quilted by Lois Lambert.

Stencil painting on dark fabric can sometimes give added problems. It is best to use a palette of light colors. The paint just seems to sink into the dark fabric and disappear, so you will find yourself going back over many areas to bring up the quality of lightness of the colors you wish to create. Some stencilers make it a practice to first apply a base coat of white paint and then add their desired color. This method builds up the paint and will make a drastic change in the surface of the fabric, causing it to become stiff. Only outline quilting of the designs is used because the needle cannot penetrate the painted area. Quilt all borders in the ditch. For this quilt design I took the liberty to substitute holly leaves in the old applique design of Oak Leaf and Reel. The wide white border echos the white shading in the leaf design making the contrast of light and dark very interesting. Parallel quilting lines, simulating patchwork pieced seams, surround each stenciled design.

THE CHRISTMAS ROSE
52½" x 64" patchwork quilt with stenciled design.

A gift of a single red rose, redolent and beautiful beyond words, is a romantic act to be cherished at the holiday season. This Christmas Rose quilt could recall such fond memories. The placement of the long-stemmed roses in this design cause a continual movement that creates a regal feeling. The dark green sashing makes a firm statement of a majestic accent. I have worked a running stitch of red perle embroidery floss to form the graceful oval outlines after they have been quilted. Adding short cut yarn tufts gives the quilt a very feminine touch. Many quilt judges frown on such embellishments, but to me the tufting gives a tactile dimension to the quilt obtainable in no other way. The very thin outer dark green border repeats the delicate feeling of the rose design. Note that the wide bridges in the stencil leaves are not quilted, keeping the leaves as a large puffed area. All other parts of the stencil are outline quilted. The sashing and borders are quilted in the ditch.

GREEN POINSETTIAS
37" x 49" whole-cloth quilt with stenciled design.

I found this Indian Arrowhead quilt design about ten years ago in an "Aunt Martha's" quilt leaflet (No. 3540) and pieced it with bright red and white flag fabric I found in a yard goods outlet store in the South. I could not pass this quilt design by for this collection, the eight-pointed flowers were a natural excuse for making a Green Poinsettia quilt. The little red center dots spell Christmas. The design is so powerful with its clean precise cut lines, and its eye teasing pattern, it has remained one of my favorites. Adapting a stencil for this design was easy, but the painting a real challenge. The simple stencil is turned every which way. The only way I could keep ahead of myself was to refer back to the illustration. I suggest you have your book open when you start to paint. Painted fabric is hard to quilt, so I just avoided the large green areas and concentrated on quilting the white fabric to keep things under control with inch wide rows of stitches. The ditch of the red border was quilted.

HEARTS AND FLOWERS

HEARTS AND FLOWERS
54" x 65½" patchwork quilt with stenciled design. Quilted by Lois Lambert.

A combination of flowers and hearts has been a favorite subject of quiltmakers for generations. The placement of the hearts in this quilt form a solid core for each quilt block. Flowers, looking very much like Christmas poinsettias, repeat the color and balance the red hearts and are all well contained within the bright red sashing frame. The simple pattern of the leaves moving in a lively circle hold all in place and add a repetition of the dark green sashing. A touch of yellow-green for the center of the flowers gives a variety in the value and intensity of the colors. The two long light sashing strips in the middle of the quilt appear to make the quilt longer than it really is. The stencil designs were outline quilted. Sashing and borders are quilted in the ditch.

THE FIRST NOEL
24" x 31" whole-cloth quilt with pieced borders and stenciled design.
Quilted by Lois Lambert.

The religious theme with its symbolic figures is a tradition of the Christmas season. I have worked my design of this Nativity panel to emphasize the creche by placing the kneeling figure with its dark protruding arm close to the child. The diagonal line of the figures behind the crib also pull the attention to the Christ child. Note how I have made full use of the bridges in the design of the figures to accent the rhythmic flow of their robes. My color scheme is muted and reflects the more reverent side of the holidays, yet the multicolored clothing of the wise men and shepherds give a faithful hint to their original hues. The bridges provide a space for quilting lines giving more accent to the outline quilting of the figures. The waffle quilting fills the background. The lack of bright reds and greens is reason enough to keep this wallhanging on display long after the yuletide days.

CHRISTMAS TREATS
45" x 51½" patchwork quilt with stenciled design.

After finishing the stenciling on this quilt top, I was taken back by its appearance. It was hard to believe I had made such a busy quilt. But after living with it for awhile, I now look on it as a very colorful, spirited accent for the holidays. The wide green and white polka dot sashing is subdued somewhat by the intersecting white squares of the sashing that are quilted with a bold X, identical to those in the outer white border. Little dark green diamond shapes with a few red dots form an irregular octagon halo around the fruit baskets. The stencil shading on the baskets started with a light area of yellow ochre and were worked over with dark brown. The red berries painted in a rather solid fashion were delicately shaded with a "dirty" raw umber brush. Outline quilting of the baskets portrays a true form and the berries plump a little when quilted, adding a special dimension. Sashing and borders are quilted in the ditch. The quilt takes on a happy-go-lucky feeling, welcomed anytime of the year.

LAUREL ROSE
63½" x 84½" whole-cloth quilt with stenciled design.

I like this quilt. Its bright red and green color combination sends out an aroma that smells like Christmas peppermint sticks and pine trees. The crisp white background fabric of this whole-cloth quilt is perfect as a glamorous contrast for the colors. The classic repetition of the components of the inner design touching each other and creating other designs within themselves, gives the eye a profusion of busywork. The quilt design is delightfully organized which demanded careful draftmanship. My master plan started in the center of the quilt and grew outwards. Accurate measuring was the key. The stencil painting was easily performed once everything had been marked for placement. The football-shaped quilting lines around the red flowers create a design of their own and become an integral part of the overall plan of the quilt. All stenciled designs are outline quilted, including the sawtooth dark green border design. This quilt was displayed at the 1989 AQS Quilt Show. (Extra quilting was added.)

CARDINALS IN A PEAR TREE
30½" x 30½" patchwork quilt with stenciled design.

This small patchwork wallhanging was designed with a tongue-in-cheek attitude, being a take-off from the "Partridge in a Pear Tree" holiday song. I thought a red cardinal would make a joyous addition to the Christmas decor. Birds, branches and leaves have a semblance of folk art qualities. The five large diamond quilt blocks, set on the points, contribute to the interest of the design while the narrow red sashing places all within a frame. Rows of horizontal and vertical quilting stitches 1¼" apart make the outer plain triangles more attractive. The stencil designs are all outline quilted. Sashing and borders are quilted in the ditch.

SANTAS BIG AND LITTLE
45" x 62½" patchwork quilt with stenciled design. Quilted by Lois Lambert.

Repetition, repetition is the word for this vibrant quilt. The identical Santas standing in a row are just as important to the overall design of the quilt as the Santas standing in the windows. I talk about brilliant flickering reds and greens in the color wheel section of this book. This quilt is a perfect example of using colors side-by-side with the same intensity and value. The light red in the plaid sashing is the only saving factor; they do keep the bright red and green fabric under control. I wanted to keep a unity with the plaid fabric so I cut all the sashing strips in exactly the same way. Each Santa is outline quilted with black thread, a departure from tradition, but giving the Santas a roundness of stature with a coloring book cutout accent. The ditches of the plain fabric are quilted with red thread.

HOLLY WREATH
62½" x 75" patchwork quilt with stenciled design.

The large oversized holly leaf circle gives this quilt a bold holiday feeling. A stencil design consisting of just three holly leaves is repeated three times to form the wreath. Wide bridges create the accent for the center vein of each leaf. Outline quilting of the leaves gives an honest clue to nature. The two circles of quilting stitches complete the fullness of the wreath. All sashing and borders are quilted in the ditch. Extra off-white sashing spacers extend the length of the quilt. A photo of this Holly Wreath quilt made a nice Christmas card for me a year ago.

SCARLET RIBBONS

46½" x 57½" patchwork quilt with stenciled design.

Colors of light and dark, bright and dull, all counterbalance each other to shape the distinguishing design of this quilt. The red ribbon, with its thick and thin contours, sets the action for each quilt block. The traditional holly leaf supplies the essences for the gala day celebration. The stencils are all painted in a solid technique. Rows of quilting stitches are worked along the center of the sashing strips and diagonally across the corners of each quilt block to create an octagon design. The ribbons are outline quilted, but the holly leaves are just quilted on the bridge areas. All the ditches are quilted.

THE COMING AND THE GOING
42½" x 45½" patchwork quilt with stenciled design.

This happy little pictorial wallhanging reflects the whimsical side of the festive days of Christmas. An amusing version of a one horse sleigh could snap back a memory or two of years gone by. The typical color scheme of red and green is boldly accented by the dashing black horses. The black repeat of the quilt binding brings all things together. Outline quilting sets off the subjects and is substantiated by long horizontal quilting rows on the white background. I pieced the quilt top before stencil painting. This small quilt with its artistically grouped horses and sleighs has a definite rural flavor.

LOVING HEARTS

43½" x 58" patchwork quilt with stenciled design.

When the parts of a stencil design become smaller in scale, as in this quilt design, the overall perception becomes dainty. Here the large delicate center areas are nicely balanced with the larger red hearts that hold their own place next to the wide dark green sashing. The quilt blocks set in a most traditional way present each design in a very organized plan. Quilting is held to a minimum, only appearing on the large hearts and stems and around the green center motif. All sashing and borders are quilted in the ditch.

BRIGHT STAR
45" x 61½" whole-cloth quilt with stenciled design.

The red stars in this quilt are identified as an old favorite quilt design called the Mariner's Compass. This pattern gained much popularity in the 1840's, especially in New England. My design weaves an interesting motif which uses unstenciled fabric to create a hexagon shape reminiscent of the Grandmother's Flower Garden quilt design. I positioned the blue stars so the points would touch each other forming the hexagons. For the blue stars I used a one-inch stencil brush and pulled the brush strokes from the outer edge of the stencil opening in toward the center with little or no care given to controlling the streaking of the paint, thus creating a technique of its own. The red star design was superimposed over the blue and painted in a solid manner. The inner hexagon areas of the red stars were outline quilted. The larger hexagons between the blue stars are quilted ¼" from the blue stencil.

Various and Sundry Quilt Thoughts

I had an art teacher in grade school that made a big impression on me. She had a brown fur coat, wore rose-tinted glasses and she taught me how to make a stencil. I can hear her now - "A stencil is just a fancy hole cut from a piece of paper." Her explanations have had a long lasting influence on me. The countless number of stencils I have made since those school days have been done with such ease and assurance. Now that my stencils have found a place on my quilts, I'm not sure I make a quilt for the quilt's sake or for the fun I have stenciling the quilt. Which ever way, it adds up to a feeling of fulfillment.

The reason for making a quilt may find its source in most any facet of life. There are more than a profusion of reasons to inspire and motivate you to envision a quilt. Being exposed to other quilts is most likely the prime source of inspiration. Seeing what someone else has actually done and how it was done is a prompter to set the imagination in a whirl.

Looking and seeing what you are looking at leads you to balance and compare in your mind as to how the idea might look in such-and-such a color or how it would fit into that particular choice spot, is all a part of being motivated, being inspired. Bits and pieces of color and design will speak out to you and you will discover just what you will want to discard. You are formulating your likes and dislikes. Will it be a whole-cloth stenciled quilt or will it follow the more traditional techniques of patchwork? Where will it be used and who will be using it? If a quilt is to be made for a special person, the love of giving is the most sincere reason you could possibly have for making the quilt. As these thoughts all simmer down and the dross is skimmed, your plans will finally take shape.

The quilter who becomes enthralled with the stenciled quilt will never be the same. I like to think of a stenciled quilt as being an extension of traditional quiltmaking or an unfolding of a profound idea that transcends a typical applique or patchwork quilt. The thoughts of such an idea are endless.

A stenciled quilt can reflect any mode or draft of patchwork or applique procedures. Color schemes and design textures are at your fingertips. Truly, I know of no bounds that could hamper you from portraying your wildest concepts of a quilt by the use of stencils.

In making my plans for the quilts in this Christmas collection, I thought it best to make smaller quilts to be used as wallhangings. A smaller project is always welcomed at the busy holiday time. I wondered about using these quilts as bed covers, the seasonal colors of bright red and green are not the most popular colors for a bedroom.

When you study these quilts and stencil patterns, let your imagination wander and try to visualize how they would look in another color combination. All the stencil patterns in this book can be adjusted to any size quilt.

The designing of a stencil pattern can be unconstrained and structured. The cutting of a stencil is readily comprehended, and as you will see, the skills of stencil painting are easily accomplished with a little practice.

A stenciled quilt adheres strictly to the old time-honored ways of assembling and quilting a quilt, but as stated, the stenciled quilt takes you beyond the perimeter of traditional quiltmaking.

Thinking in the line of tradition, as the handing down of information, I am reminded of my grandmother. So many times I watched her as she held her sewing needle up to the light in readiness to pierce the thread through the eye of the needle. To me this was just the only way to do it.

Then one day as I was teaching my third graders to thread their needles in preparation for a sewing lesson, and at this point in time I was not being very successful, I thought perhaps there must be a better way for them to thread their needles, a different way, but not neccessarily a new way. So I had the children hold the cut end of the thread between their thumb and first finger with just the very tip end of the thread showing and then had them place the eye of the needle over the end of the thread. Well, it worked! I had many happy faces expressing such a feeling of satisfaction and accomplishment.

This now in turn reminds me of a story of a young bride who was preparing dinner. As she cut off both ends of the ham, her husband asked why she did that. She replied that it was a special little trick her mother had always done. The bewildered husband then asked his mother-in-law why she had cut the ham in this way, and her reply was

that her mother had always done it. Then the husband asked the grandmother, and with an almost disgusting look, said she cut the ends off of the ham so it would fit into the roasting pan.

How many times have we allowed ourselves to be taken in with such unwarranted advice? The history of quiltmaking is ingrained with folklore that sometimes needs to be reexamined. We must be alert to changing ways and have an open mind, as an individual, to make use of any new technique that will make us a better quilter.

Sharing is a unique fragment of quiltmaking. Sharing bits and scraps of fabric and seeing them worked into a lovely patched or appliqued quilt design has been the bond of many beautiful and lasting friendships. Old quilt designs handed down from one generation to another among families has promoted strong family traditions. A grandmother seeing that each girl in the family receives a quilt of a particular design, like the one made for her by her grandmother when she was a little girl, or likewise for the boys in the family - a quilt designed like the one Grampa took with him when he was allowed to sleep in the hay loft - are customs worth keeping.

A quilt means warmth, something to cuddle you, to comfort you. Something to hold close. It is no wonder that a quilt has long been considered a precious possession. The touch of the soft fabric and the sight of the thousands and thousands of tiny quilting stitches is mind-boggling and the wonder of hours spent in creating such a work of art.

How sad it is to see the remnants of what was a beautiful quilt wrapped around a greasy lawn mower in the back of a station wagon. I'm sure we have all seen situations that parallel this. If only there had been a love and appreciation for someone else's time and dedication to this most noteworthy art form it would have never happened.

Thinking about why the person made the quilt, how it was inspired, where the fabric came from, when and where it was made, who were the people who slept under it, could be unanswered questions. Quilt lore is fascinating, if at times it is only fabricated. We all have our own ways of choosing and repeating what we often fantasize in a special quilt. Researching the true facts and expounding on them is certainly better than just "cutting off both ends of the ham!"

If you have become obsessed with quilting it won't be long before you will be making plans for a place of your own where you can stash your array of fabrics and quilting supplies. This place will become your special hide-a-way where you can think and plan.

In the studio loft of my Victorian cottage home, circa 1884, where I quilt, the radio is tuned softly to a FM music station. The view from my large picture window looks through the huge red pines out to West Grand Traverse Bay just a few miles from the 45th parallel. The little sewing rocker I sit in was one my grandmother rocked me in as a small child. The old scrub-top table I use as a writing desk is distressed with knife marks and grease stains from cooking oils. The shelf above the table holds small precious photos of family members and above all this is a watercolor painting I made many years ago of a century old farm house which is now the studio home for the "Twiggery" belonging to my nephew.

I rarely throw anything away so I have great quantities of memorabilia which I keep in order. I just think of it as organized clutter. What fond memories are suggested to me by these treasures, an endless source of inspiration for all my artwork, including my quilts. When I am in my studio, I am in another world. It is my own place to live my own thoughts.

During my many years as an art teacher, I have established a few guidelines for evaluating my students. I always look for and stress originality in my student's work and strive to have them seek out their own ideas. Exposure to other quilts does not have to be a requisite to create a good stenciled quilt design. The basic elements of good design can be their only reference.

I dwell only on the good qualities of the student's work, be it design or needle craftsmanship, perfecting the obvious. Patience and encouragement for a beginning stenciler or quilter is the "wonder-worker." The moment my students gain a good degree of confidence, I can stand aside and watch, letting their own reassurance take over. What a joy to experience someone else's delights!

Making and Painting Your Own Stencil

with an

Outline of General Instructions

Making and Painting Your Own Stencil

Stencils have been in use for thousands of years. Fragments of cave paintings have been found dating to the Stone Age suggesting stencils had been used. The Egyptians stencil painted their mummy cases. Both the Chinese and Japanese stenciled silk fabrics and lavishly embroidered them with silk and metallic threads. Primitive South Pacific Island women used large tropical leaves for making stencils to dye paint their fabrics. Medieval churches in England and throughout Europe were stencil painted with endless borders of designs in rich colors and adorned with the addition of gold leaf. Many times the stencils were incorporated with freehand paintings of figures often applied to wood panels. The English makers of stenciled wallpapers in the mid-1700's were the most prominent users of stencils up to this date.

Old manuscripts were illustrated with the use of stencils. The stencil mania reached its peak during the Victorian era. Mansions and theaters were enveloped with an array of stencils which never before had been matched. This list could go on and on.

Stencils are versatile. They adapt well to so many different art forms. Stenciled quiltmaking today is just now becoming a long overlooked art form. Quilts are still important as bed covers, but are becoming more important as a commercial display of art.

Are you ready to become involved? Gather your thoughts about a design for a stenciled quilt and let's get started!

Once you have decided upon a drawing for your stencil, whether it is your own or one to be copied, it must be reworked to make it become a good stencil. A stencil must maintain a structural strength when the stencil openings are cut away. This means there must be "bridges," (sometimes called ladders), left between the openings of the design. Bridges are spacers of stencil material that give support to the open cut design.

In reworking the design, draw the shapes of the design to be cut away and make allowances for many bridges. These bridges will become a very important and distinguishing part of the design. If the bridges are wide, they will confirm a bold feeling for the design. If the bridges are thin, the concept will be light and delicate. Experiment with the same design using wide and thin bridges to see which will convey the impression you wish to create. I have found it more rewarding to stay with one size bridge throughout a design. It establishes a unity and rhythm, especially if the design is repeated over and over again. The stencil designs in this book have all been prepared with bridges.

Transferring the drawing to the stencil material can be done in several ways. If the stencil material is semi-transparent, simply overlay it on the drawing and trace with a pencil or marking pen. If the stencil material is opaque, such as cardboard, the drawing must be transferred with carbon paper. All drawings must make allowances for at least 1½" margin of stencil material surrounding the design. This margin will prevent the stencil brush from smudging the surrounding fabric.

The stencil material I prefer is semi-transparent frosted Mylar™, gauge .05 mil. This material has a see-through quality that is very helpful when drawing the design and makes easy placement when painting. Mylar™ can be obtained from architectural supply companies or art craft stores. It is a tough plastic easily cut with a utility knife or a single edge razor blade. I prefer cutting my stencils with small sharp pointed embroidery scissors. A small slit in the plastic within the design area with a single edge razor blade enables me to maneuver the small scissors with ease. If the razor blade becomes dull, discard it.

When using a cutting tool, hold it in your hand as you would a pencil. Pierce the plastic with the point of the cutting tool on the pencil line of the design. The knife hand stays in the same position while the other hand gently moves the plastic to negotiate the cut. When not using this method make sure you always pull the cutting blade toward you. If a miss cut should occur just patch it with a piece of transparent tape. Cut all the small areas of the design first, which are the hardest to cut, and save the larger areas for last. This method of work will help to maintain the original strength of the stencil material for a longer period. Stencils made of Mylar™ are very durable and can be easily cleaned with shellac thinner for reuse. For a cutting base cover the edges of a 9" x 12" piece of glass with masking tape.

Each stencil makes its own demands. It is sometimes wise to cut separate stencils if more than one color is used, especially if the design is

complex and the different color areas are close to each other. On more simple stencils that call for several colors, the stencil openings can be covered over with masking tape when not in use. If the stickiness of the tape in the stencil opening is a problem, just dust with a little baby powder. When making subsequent stencils, always return to the original drawing and trace with extreme accuracy to align the design correctly. For separate color stencils, trace the full design for each stencil sheet to insure true registration. Always mark TOP on each stencil.

Painting! This is the real fun part of making a stenciled quilt. Seeing your stencil design come alive in colors that blend with the mood you wish to create is pure delight. Dark bold colors interspersed with light flashes of bright intense colors will certainly capture the excitement of the Christmas season. Painting with such spirited colors can positively lift one's morale.

Painting has always been an important activity for me. My master's degree work was done in watercolor painting and I thought at that point in my life, it was the ultimate technique. As the years have passed, my interests have moved from one art phase to another. Stencil painting quilts is a far substitute for watercolor painting, but the enjoyment of manipulating paint and brush is an everlasting infatuation. Even now, as I am in my "quiltmaking period," I have not had to put my paint brush down. That is reason enough for me to be engrossed with stencil painted quilts.

Stencil painting *is* easy, and don't let anyone intimidate you by telling you differently. Even my dear little grade school children mastered stenciling techniques. Do not feel modest about experimenting with color either. Sometimes innocence is the prompter of a very lovely work of art.

Individual quilt blocks can be stenciled before they are set into the quilt top. If you are a little timid about making mistakes with the paint, this may be a good way to start, to build your confidence.

I like to complete all the patchwork first and paint directly on the finished quilt top. This way I know my stencils will be exactly centered in each block. I have always said if I did make a painting mistake, I could always rip out that block and stitch in a new one. Fortunately for me, I have not had to do this. See - fabric stenciling is easy!

Work with just one color at a time. Place a large blob of paint on the palette, perhaps a half spoon full. Dip the stencil brush into the edge of the paint and draw only a small amount out onto the center of the palette. Work the paint into the end of the brush making sure it has a sparce amount of paint evenly distributed on the flat end. The big secret of being a good stenciler is knowing how to control the amount of paint on the brush. A very little paint goes a long way. When you master this, you will never have problems of blotchy paint spots or paint seeping under the stencil. If you are not sure about the amount of paint on the brush, just test it on a scrap of fabric. Don't let this become a habit, this is a very wasteful way to paint.

Stencil brushes come is six sizes. No. 4 (3/8"), No. 8 (1/2"), and 1" are popular sizes. Remember the larger the brush, the more paint is required, and the more paint used at a given time takes more skill to manipulate.

A good stencil painting does not mean the colors are painted in solid. This technique is reserved for adding smaller accents of dark or bright colors. Other techniques that leave the fabric showing through the paint, as I think of as breathing spaces in the fabric, can create striking effects. Pouncing the brush creates a stippling effect. Streaking or stroking, sometimes called feathering, makes stripes that often show movement. Shading can be created with a second color by streaking or feathering the colors or using a circular motion that creates a feeling of roundess. The use of stenciling props, chicken wire, hardware cloth, plastic onion bags stretched in an embroidery hoop, window screen and extruded metal can all produce the effects of printed patterns on the fabric.

The actual painting of a stencil is done by working the stencil brush from the Mylar™ into the stencil opening. In reproducing many painted stencils of one design, you will find they are similar, but each one will seem to have its own identity.

The first stencil to be painted should be the one with the largest cut openings, making the following stencils easier to place for correct registration. Stenciling quilt blocks should present no problems in centering the design within the block. For a whole-cloth quilt top, the stencil painting should start in the center of the fabric and worked out to the edges. Before doing any stencil painting on a whole-cloth, I always do a lot of measuring and planning to make sure my stencil pattern will come out even. True outer edge measurements and folded press crease lines must be perfect. Many times I will mark, with a watercolor fabric marker,

the entire quilt top at points where each stencil will butt up to the next stencil. With all this pre-planning behind me, I can concentrate on the fun of painting. Stay alert and try to anticipate any problems before they ever happen when you are painting. I'm sure these few tips will make you a very good stenciler.

*** Mylar™ is a trademark of the DuPont Co. and is the preferred working material of the author.**

Stencil Painting Techniques

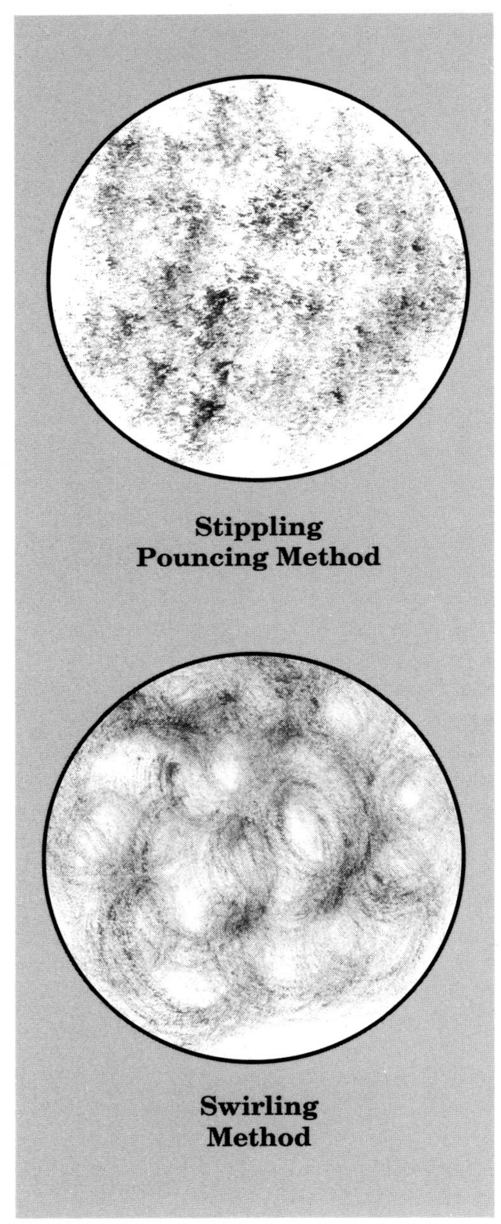

Stippling Pouncing Method

Swirling Method

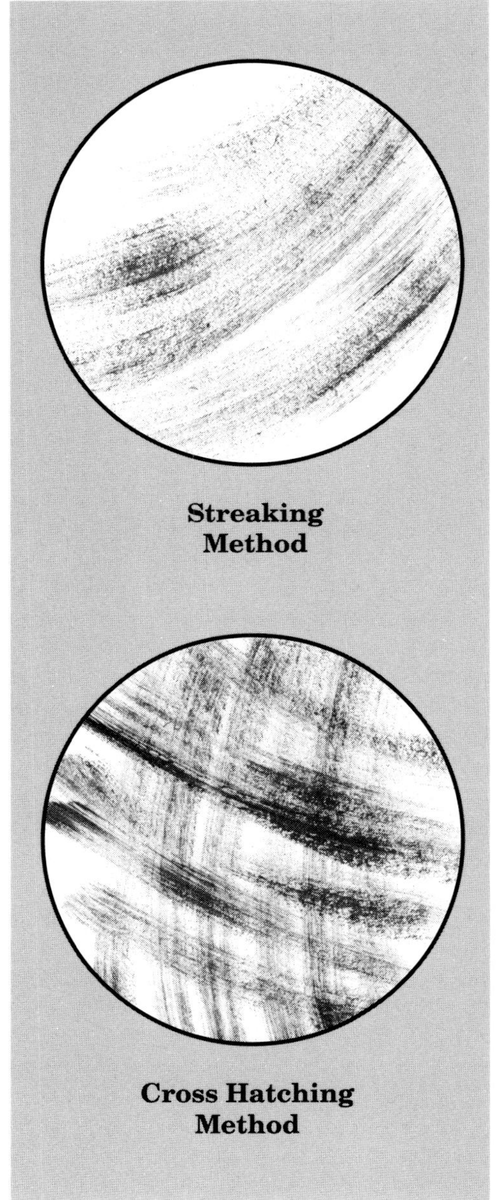

Streaking Method

Cross Hatching Method

Stenciling Props

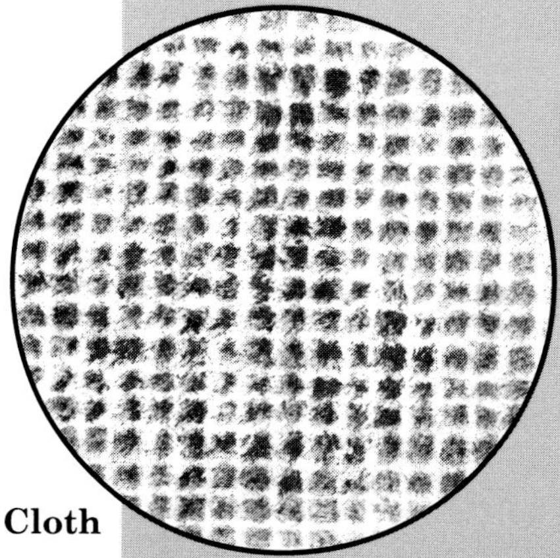

1/8" Hardware Cloth

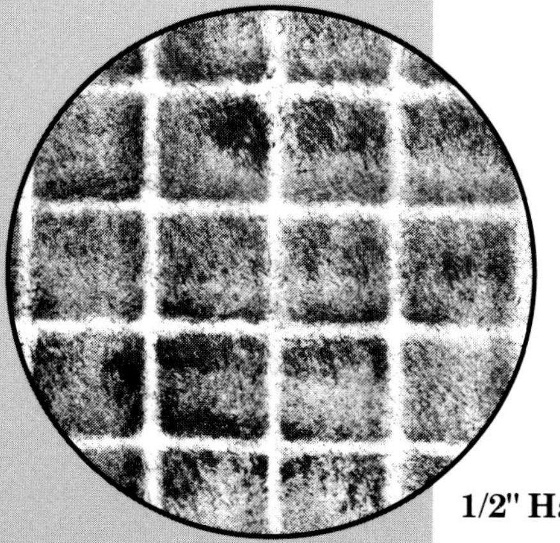

1/2" Hardware Cloth

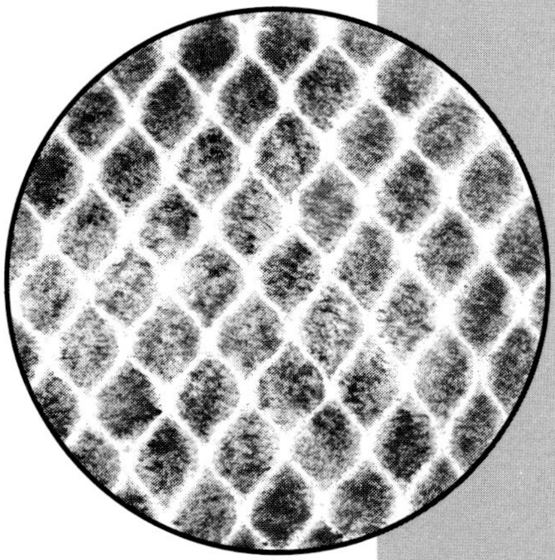

Plastic Onion Bag

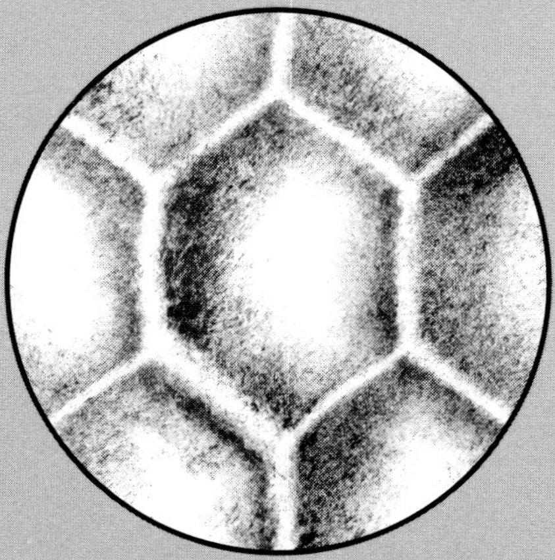

Chicken Wire

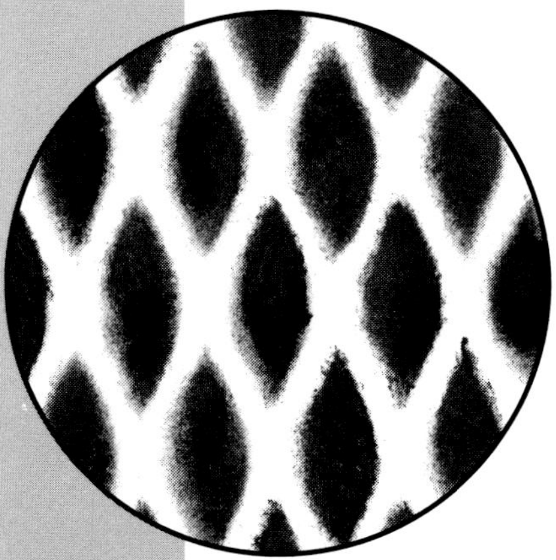

Extruded Metal

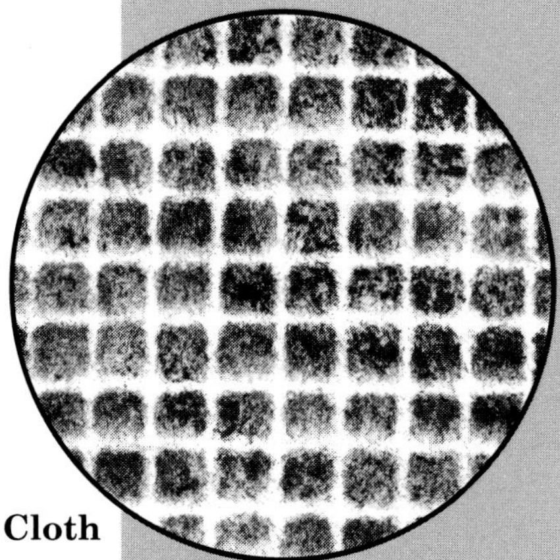

1/4" Hardware Cloth

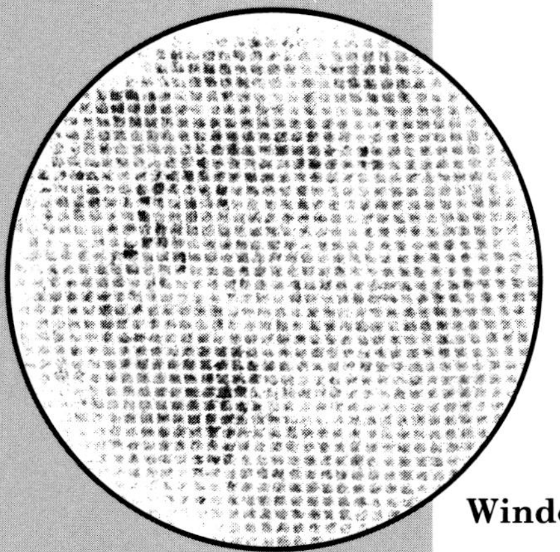

Window Screen

Using The Color Wheel

The traditional Christmas colors of red and green are hard to beat! Red, being the most advancing color on the color wheel sets the stage for the excitement of the season.

Red is a primary color and cannot be made from other colors, but has to be manufactured with chemicals, as is also true of the other primary colors of blue and yellow. Usually the Christmas red is a very bright intense color. If the eye is allowed to become saturated with this intense red, an after-image of green is seen. This after-image is a common response for all complementary colors, colors lying opposite to each other on the color wheel.

We often see red and green used side-by-side in Christmas decor that create a visual pulsation or flickering. The explanation for this lies in the fact that both the red and green are equal in intensity, or contain the same amount of brightness. We can say they have the same value and the same intensity. The value of a color deals with the lightness and darkness, while the intensity of a color deals with the brightness or dullness. The word "hue" is another name for color.

Because red and green are complementary colors they can work for each other in subduing each other. A little green will kill the intensity of red, and vice versa. To alter the brightness of any color just add a bit of the complementary color. Avoid using black to tone down a color because the color will become muddy looking. Complementary colors always help to keep mixed colors looking fresh and clean.

To reap the full enjoyments of stencil painting you will need to understand some simple math concerning the color wheel. Here I have reduced the facts to their lowest denominator. Mixing colors can be great fun when you learn these basics.

The Color Wheel

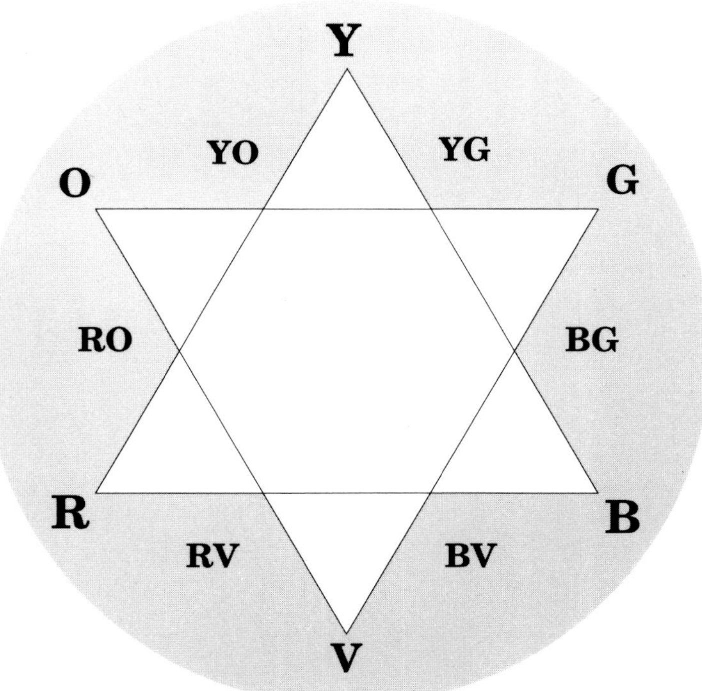

Primary Colors		Secondary Colors	Intermediate Colors
Red + Yellow	=	Orange	Y + O = Yellow Orange
Yellow + Blue	=	Green	Y + G = Yellow Green
Blue + Red	=	Violet	B + G = Blue Green
			B + V = Blue Violet
			R + V = Red Violet
			R + O = Red Orange
Blue + Orange = Brown			
Red + Yellow + Blue = Black			

We have talked about bright intense colors and how to dull them down, now we can consider light or pastel colors. To make a color lighter in value (and we are speaking of latex or acrylic paints that will be used for our stencil painting on fabric), white paint must be added to a color. This is truly the way people say it, but the actual mixing of the paint must be done in just the opposite way. Always add small amounts of color to the white paint or else you can end up with an enormous amount of mixed color, wasting large quantities of white paint.

Now our color discussion takes us a step farther in knowing how to use colors in a schematic way. These color schemes presented are structured in accord with the color wheel and as I comment on them it may be well for you to refer back to the color wheel. Formulated color combinations can take the fret and worry out of planning a color coordinated quilt. Start with your color preference first and fit that color into a given scheme to arrive at a harmonious balance with the other new colors.

In selecting a distinctive color scheme, it is necessary to consider color, value and intensity. These three properties must be in accord to create a blending that will give your quilt a delightful glow.

Analogous Scheme: Two to four colors adjacent to each other on the color wheel. Sometimes referred to as neighboring colors. Example: yellow, yellow green, green, blue green.

Complementary Scheme: Any two colors that lie directly opposite each other on the color wheel. Example: red and green, blue and orange, yellow and violet.

Split Complementary Scheme: Three colors. One complementary color is used while the other complementary color is replaced with the two intermediate colors on either side of it. Example: red, yellow green, blue green.

Double Split Complementary Scheme: Four colors. Basing the scheme on two complementary colors but not using either, rather using the two intermediate colors on either side of them. Example: yellow orange, yellow green and red violet, blue violet.

Monochromatic Scheme: One single color with diverse values and intensities. Example: dark dull red, medium bright red, light red fading to pink.

Triad Scheme: Three colors plotted on an equal triangle on the color wheel. Example: red, yellow, blue.

Working and experimenting with colors is rewarding and can extend far beyond just a means of aiding the effectiveness of stencil work. Your newly discovered color schemes can be of great assistance in selecting your personal choice of fashions and home decor. Colors are the brightener of life.

Outline of General Instructions

*** Mylar™ is a trademark of the DuPont Co. and is the preferred working material of the author. Within these instructions, reference is made to plastic sheets as a stencil making material. The author uses Mylar™ in construction of her stencils.**

Materials for Making a Stenciled Quilt:

- Fabric of choice for quilt top and backing, size to be considered
- Batting - cotton, wool or polyester fiber
- Quilting needles, thread and thimble
- Water soluble fabric marking pen
- Iron, ironing board
- 14" wooden quilting hoop
- Drawing paper, pencil
- 9" x 12" piece of plate glass for a cutting base (taped edges)
- Single edge razor blades or utility knife
- Small, sharp pointed embroidery or manicure scissors
- Plastic sheets, with one side frosted
- Masking tape and transparent tape
- Plastic butter carton lid for palette
- Water jar, bath towel paint rags
- #4 round stencil brush is good starting size
- A choice of acrylic or latex interior or exterior decorator paint, artist tube (acrylic or latex) paint, small jars or squeeze bottles of acrylic craft paint
- Shellac thinner

Designing the Quilt Stencil:

- The design must conform to the given size of the quilt block. Allow a fabric margin of ½" to 1" on all sides of the quilt block which would include a ¼" seam allowance.
- The design may be symmetrical or asymmetrical and should be planned with the idea of being repeated in a harmonious way.
- The setting of the quilt blocks will dictate the construction and position of the stencil design. A whole-cloth quilt may be designed with block patterns and stenciled sashing, as an overall design, or as a medallion-style quilt with stenciled borders.
- The consideration of a color scheme may influence the planning of a design.

Making the Stencil:

- Overlay the plastic sheet on the completed quilt block design or whole-cloth design, tape in place and trace with a pencil on the frosted side.
- A 1½" margin of plastic should extend beyond the design on all 4 sides.
- Make a complete drawing on the plastic for each color stencil. This makes registration of the colors easy.
- Mark TOP on top edge of the plastic sheets.
- Cut a separate stencil for each color to be used.
- Place plastic sheet on glass cutting base and prepare to cut with a single-edge razor blade or utility knife.
- Discard blade when dull.
- Pierce the corner of the blade through the plastic.
- Hold blade hand steady and move the plastic into the blade with the palm of the other hand.
- Small parts and curves of the design can be cut with the embroidery or manicure scissors.
- Cut the smaller parts of the design first, to maintain the original structural strength of the plastic stencil for a longer period.
- A paper punch or leather punch makes good dots.
- Miscuts can be easily patched with transparent tape.
- A stencil painting is only as good as the cut stencil.
- Store clean cut stencils in a flat folder.

Preparation of the Quilt Top:

- All fabric must be washed to remove sizing, and pressed to remove wrinkles.
- All fabric should be of the same weight containing a low thread count (number of threads per inch). Bed sheets with 120 to 150 thread count can be used. Do not use fine percale fabric.
- If possible, use 100% cotton fabric or fabric with a high percent of cotton.
- Trim selvage edges.

- Sashing and border strips should be cut from the fabric first so there will be no unnecessary piecing.
- Cut all sashing and border strips longer than given measurements, to be trimmed when stitched. This compensates for the variation of seams. Quilt blocks can be cut from the remaining fabric.
- Fabric requirements are based on the length of the longest border strip. Some quilts will have an excess of unused fabric. Good for starting your next quilt.
- Whole-cloth quilt fabric must be precisely squared up and the outer edges trimmed to make a perfect rectangle.
- Fold fabric and press with warm iron to make crease guidelines for stencil placement on whole-cloth top.
- Press patchwork fabric as you advance from one step to another. Take care not to stretch the fabric.
- Seams should be pressed to one side onto the darker fabric.
- Seam allowance is ¼".
- The pressure foot on the sewing machine can be used for a seam allowance guide.

Options for Stenciled Quilt Tops:

- Stencil paint quilt blocks before setting them into the quilt top.
- Setting the quilt blocks and completing the quilt top before stenciling.
- Planning a full repeat layout of the stencil design for a whole-cloth quilt top.
- The choice is a matter of preference.

Stencil Painting on Fabric:

- Painting on fabric is easier than other surfaces.
- Acrylic and latex paints dry almost immediately to the touch enabling the stencil to be moved over freshly painted area.
- The paint should penetrate the surface of the fabric, but should not ooze out on the back side.
- Acrylic or latex paint must be heat set into the fabric.
- Establish a painting technique before proceeding to the good fabric.

Techniques:

- Pouncing is an up and down motion of the brush and creates a stippling effect.
- Streaking or stroking the brush creates a variety of painted stripes, nice for creating a feeling of movement.
- Circular motion is a steady contact of the brush to the fabric and will produce a simple way of shading colors.
- A combination of these techniques give interesting results.
- Once a technique is established, stick with it so the stenciling will have a feeling of consistency.

Stenciling Props:

- Unique textures can be created by stenciling through props such as chicken wire, hardware cloth, plastic onion bags stretched in an embroidery hoop, window screen and extruded metal.

Painting the Stencil:

- Protect the table surface, the paint may seep through the fabric.
- Tape the stencil to the fabric.
- A #4 stencil brush is easy to handle.
- Larger brushes use more paint and could present problems.
- Place a small amount of paint on the plastic lid palette.
- Work a small amount of paint into the brush.
- Practice painting on scrap fabric.
- Pounce the brush up and down on a scrap of fabric to remove extra blobs of paint.
- A little paint goes a long way.
- Move the stencil brush from the plastic into the stencil opening. This prevents the paint from going under the stencil.
- Check the back side of the stencil, keeping it free of excess paint.
- Make a proof stencil painting on practice fabric. The proof removes all pencil smudges from the plastic stencil.
- Mistakes can be corrected on the stencil at this time.
- Do not allow the paint to build up in the brush.
- If the paint becomes too thick, add a small amount of water.
- After washing a brush, work it into the terry cloth paint rag to remove all moisture.
- Place dirty paint brushes in the water jar.
- Acrylic and latex paints clean up with soap and water.
- Use shellac thinner (alcohol) to clean dry paint from plastic stencils.

Quilt Top Completion:

- Allow the paint to dry overnight.
- Heat set the color with a hot dry iron.
- Press the backside first then the front side with a pressing cloth.
- Mark all quilting lines using a watercolor marker. Always test to see if markers wash out of fabric.
- To assemble a quilt, place the backing fabric right side down, lay batting over backing and smooth out. (The night before, unwrap the batting and spread it out to relax the creases.) Place the quilt top over the batting. The batting and backing should be at least 2 inches larger than the quilt top.
- Baste all three layers together in rows 6" apart starting from the center of the quilt.
- Do not knot the basting thread. Start with a basting backstitch and end with a basting backstitch.
- Use a round 14" quilting hoop.
- To set the hoop, place the screw-clamp hoop over the place to be quilted, smoothing out the quilt top. Place the plain hoop on the underside of the quilt. Clamp the hoops together. Turn the quilt over to the backside and if the backside is wrinkled, release the hoops very carefully and smooth the backing of the quilt. Reclamp the hoops and return to the quilt top. Adjust the screw-clamp so the quilt will not slip in the hoop. Both top and bottom of the quilt should be smooth within the hoop. If the quilt is too taut, it will be hard to quilt. Do not pull on the quilt when the hoop is set, it will stretch the quilt out of shape.
- Quilting should start from the center of the quilt, working out to the borders.
- Hand quilt around all parts of the stenciled design, adding other quilting where it will enhance the quilt.
- When resetting the hoop, always include a portion that has already been quilted.
- Quilt everything within the set hoop. It is hard to quilt close to the hoop, so don't.
- Do not end off threads when the quilting design extends beyond the hoop. Remove the needle, leaving the thread attached to be threaded again when the hoop is reset.
- Always remove the hoop from the quilt when not quilting.

Hand Quilting Techniques:

- Thread the needle using an 18" thread. Knot the end and pass the needle into the quilt top on the marked quilting line, or at the edge of the painted stencil, pull through into the batting. Pull the knot into the batting. Take a small backstitch where the thread comes out of the fabric on the marked line. Begin a running stitch of in and out, gathering 3 or 4 stitches on the needle. These stitches must go through all three layers of the quilt. Pull thread through and repeat.
- The needle should touch a finger of the hand working on the underside of the quilt with each stitch taken. At the moment of contact, that finger should give slight lift to the quilt to create a rhythmic union of both hands and needle working together.
- To end off the thread, take a backstitch and send the needle through the batting about an inch and coming out on the top of the quilt. Cut thread close to fabric.
- All stitches should be consistently spaced - 8 stitches per inch apart is nice; 10 is better.
- Trim batting and backing to quilt top and bind with bias strips.
- To smooth rough pricked fingers, use an emery board.

To preserve the true heritage of your quilt you must sign your name and completion date to a rather inconspicuous place on the quilt. If you wish to be more explicit, feel free to state where the quilt was made and the occasion or for whom it was made. Script or block letters can be worked with embroidery stitches or inscribed with a black laundry marker.

Complete Instructions

For Making Christmas Quilts

These instructions are to be used with the "Outline of General Instructions" on pages 42-44. Also see photo critiques and Glossary for word explanations.

Father Christmas

28" x 28" whole-cloth quilt with stenciled design, pictured on page 12.
(Beginner)

Materials:

Quilt top:	1 - 30" square unbleached muslin
Backing:	1 - 30" square unbleached muslin
Batting:	1 - 30" square low loft batting
Binding:	3¼ yds of 3" green binding
Stencil:	3 - 9" x 12" plastic sheets
Acrylic Paint:	Dark green, bright red, medium brown, flesh

Ball point laundry marker

Quilt Top Making:

- Mark 28" x 28" on whole-cloth, to be trimmed after quilting.
- Press center crease guidelines.

Stencil Making:

- Trace complete Santa design on each plastic sheet.
- Cut face with red body stencil.
- Cut white beard and hat with brown bag and boot stencil. Green tree can be placed in an empty corner.
- Cut holly heaves and punch red dot holes, mask out adjoining areas when painting.

Stencil Painting:

- Mark 15½" circle in center of quilt top.
- Mark placement of holly leaves, stem line will follow circle line.
- Paint leaves, berries.
- Mark placement of Santa.
- Paint in solid pouncing method.
- Heat set paint.
- Mark concentric quilting lines (as seen in quilt photo) using architect's flexible curve.

Assembling and Finishing:

- Layer quilt, baste, quilt. (See photo critique.)
- Trim edges to 28".
- Add binding and bring to back of quilt and hem.

Father Christmas

Father Christmas
Garland of Holly

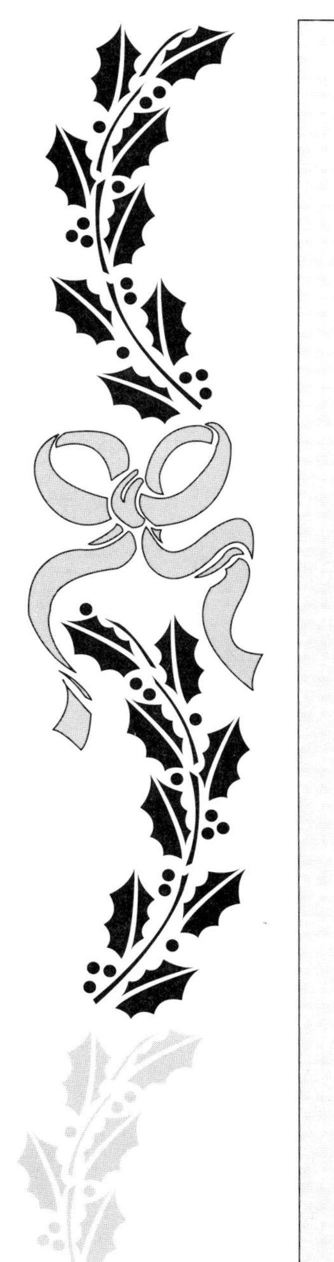

The holly pattern can be used to achieve several visual designs by changing the direction of the stencil placement. Note the examples of Father Christmas (above) and Garland of Holly (right) and their stencil placement.

Holiday Flower Garden

45" x 54½" whole-cloth quilt with stencil design, pictured on page 13.

(Intermediate)

Materials:

Quilt top:	½ white twin size sheet (take out hems)
Backing:	½ white twin size sheet (take out hems)
Batting:	Crib size
Binding:	6 yds. of green double fold commerical bias binding
Stencil:	3 - 9" x 12" plastic sheets
Acrylic paint:	Bright red, bright green, black

Quilt Top Making:

- Mark 45" x 54½" on whole-cloth, to be trimmed after quilting.
- Press center crease guidelines.

Stencil Making:

- Trace complete stencil design on plastic sheets.
- Cut separate stencils for red, green and black.

Stencil Painting:

- Mark layout of stencil design using the creased guidelines.
- Paint one color at a time, start with black.
- Paint in solid, pouncing method.
- Heat set paint.

Assembling and Finishing:

- Layer quilt, baste and quilt. (See photo critique.)
- Trim edges.
- Add binding and bring to back of quilt and hem.

Festive Lily

43½" x 43½" patchwork quilt with stencil design, pictured on page 14.
(Beginner)

Materials:

Quilt top: 1¼ yd. unbleached muslin
Sashing: 1¼ yd. red fabric
¾ yd. green fabric
Backing: 1¼ yd. of 45" unbleached muslin
Batting: 45" square
Border: Red sashing fabric
Stencil: 3 - 9" x 12" plastic sheets
Acrylic Paint: Bright red, medium green, dark green

Quilt Top Making:

- Cut 4 - 14" x 14" muslin blocks
  Cut 8 - 14" x 2" red sashing
  Cut 8 - 2" x 17" red sashing
  Cut 8 - 1½" x 17" green sashing
  Cut 8 - 1½" x 19" green sashing
  Cut 2 - 2" x 19" muslin sashing
  Cut 3 - 2" x 39" muslin sashing
  Cut 3 - 2" x 42½" muslin sashing
  Border - 3" red strips
- Frame muslin blocks with red sashing then green sashing.
- Assemble quilt top with muslin sashing.
- Add 3" red borders.

Stencil Making:

- Trace complete stencil design on plastic sheets.
- Cut a separate stencil for red, medium green and dark green.

Stencil Painting:

- Mark placement of stencil in each block corner.
- Paint one color at a time, starting with dark green.
- Paint in solid, pouncing method.
- Heat set paint.

Assembling and Finishing:

- Layer quilt, baste and quilt. (See photo critique.)
- Trim edges.
- Bring red border to quilt back and hem.

Festive Lily

Scherenschnitte

24¾" x 29¾" patchwork quilt with stenciled design, pictured on page 15.

(Intermediate)

Materials:

Quilt top:	1 yd. bright green fabric
Sashing:	1 yd. of 45" white fabric
Backing:	Use sashing fabric
Batting:	1 square yard
Border:	1 yd. bright red fabric
Stencil:	1 - 10½" x 13" plastic sheet
Acrylic Paint:	White

Quilt Top Making:

- Cut 4 - 10½" x 13" green blocks
  Cut 6 - 1½" x 13" white sashing
  Cut 3 - 1½" x 28½" white sashing
  3" red fabric
- Stitch short sashing to top and bottom of green blocks.
- Add 3" red border.

Stencil Making:

- Trace complete stencil design on plastic sheet.
- Cut stencil.

Stencil Painting:

- Paint in solid, pouncing method.
- Second painting may be necessary.
- Heat set paint.

Assembling and Finishing:

- Layer quilt, baste and quilt. (See photo critique.)
- Trim edges.
- Bring red border to back of quilt and hem.

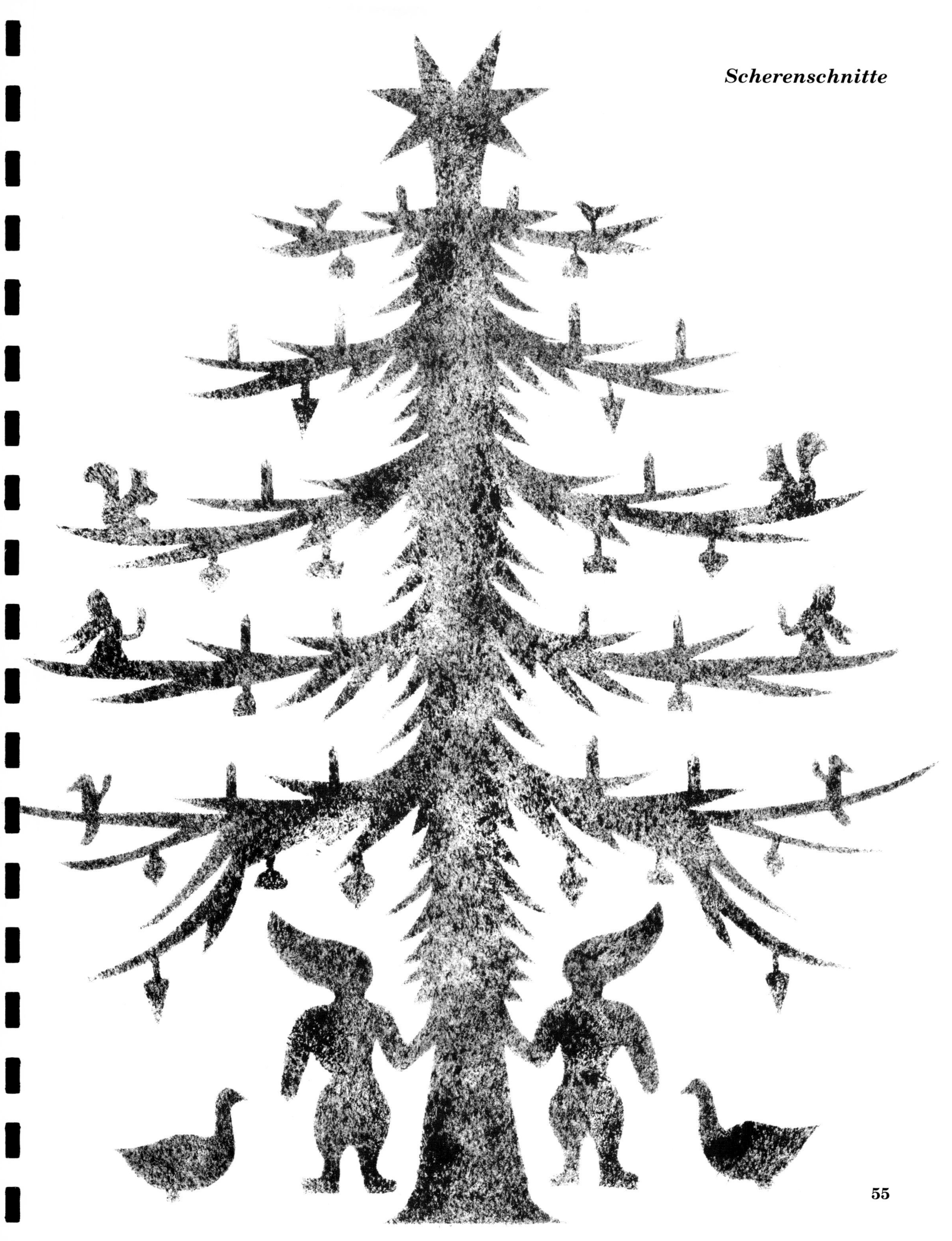

Dresden Plate

45" x 65" whole-cloth quilt with stenciled design, pictured on page 16.
(Intermediate)

Materials:

Quilt top:	1 beige color twin size sheet (take out hems)
Borders:	Use beige from top sheet
	2 yds. bright green fabric
Backing:	1 white twin size sheet (take out hems)
Batting:	1 twin size
Binding:	Use green border fabric
Stencil:	3 - 14" plastic squares
Acrylic Paint:	Bright red, bright green
Accent:	2 balls green cotton perle (D.M.C. #701)

Quilt Top Making:

- Mark 34" x 54" on beige whole-cloth.
- Cut 2 - 2" x 34" green border.
  Cut 2 - 2" x 57" green border.
  Cut 2 - 4" x 37" beige border.
  Cut 2 - 4" x 64" beige border.
  Outer border 2½" green strips.
- Add green borders to whole-cloth center.
- Add beige borders to green borders.
- Add 2½" outer green border.
- Press center crease guidelines.

Stencil Making:

- Trace complete stencil design on plastic sheets.
- See glossary for stencil pattern note.
- Tracing of design must be very accurate.
- Cut one sheet for red stencil.
- Cut one sheet for green stencil.
- Use diamond design to make border, trace and cut red and green on same sheet, mask out adjoining areas when painting.

Stencil Painting:

- Mark complete placement for stencils on whole-cloth center, use crease lines for a guide.
- Paint red stencil first, then green.
- Paint in solid, pouncing method.
- Heat set paint.

Assembling and Finishing:

- Layer quilt, baste and quilt. (See photo critique.)
- Trim edges.
- Bring outer green border to the quilt back and hem.
- Add accent of buttonhole stitch around outer and inner edge of "plate."
- Work stitch through to back side of quilt. (See glossary for buttonhole stitch.)

Dresden Plate

(See Glossary for Stencil Pattern Note)

Wedding Ring Bouquet

54" x 58" patchwork quilt with stenciled design, pictured on page 17.
(Beginner)

Materials:

Quilt top:	2 yds. white fabric
	2 yds. bright red printed fabric
Border:	Use red from top fabric
Backing:	½ white twin size sheet
Batting:	½ twin size
Binding:	6 yds. green double fold commercial bias binding
Stencil:	2 - 12" x 12" plastic sheets
Acrylic Paint:	Dark green, medium yellow-green

Quilt Top Making:

- Cut 15 - 9½" x 9½" white blocks.
  Cut 15 - 9½" x 9½" red blocks.
  Cut 2 - 2" x 48½" red border.
  Cut 2 - 2" x 54½" red border.
- Patch red and white blocks in checkerboard pattern.
- Add red border.

Stencil Making:

- Trace complete stencil design on plastic sheets.
- Cut one sheet for dark green.
- Cut one sheet for medium yellow-green.

Stencil Painting:

- Paint dark green first, then yellow-green.
- Paint in solid, pouncing method.
- Heat set paint.
- Mark quilting lines on red blocks.
- Use both green stencils as quilting templates.

Assembling and Finishing:

- Layer quilt, baste and quilt. (See photo critique.)
- Trim quilt edges.
- Add green bias binding, bring to back of quilt and hem.

Garland Of Holly

48" x 57½" patchwork quilt with stenciled design, pictured on page 18.
(Beginner)

Materials:

Quilt top:	½ white twin size sheet (take out hems)
Sashing:	1¾ yds. green fabric
Backing:	1 white twin size sheet (take out hems)
Batting:	1 twin size
Binding:	Sashing fabric
Stencil:	2 - 9" x 12" plastic sheets
Acrylic Paint:	Bright red, bright green

Quilt Top Making:

- Cut 4 - 9" x 54" white fabric panels.
  Cut 5 - 4" x 54", 3 green sashing; 2 border.
  Cut 2 - 4" x 52" green border.
- Stitch 4" sashing to 4 white panels.
- Stitch 4" green borders to top and bottom.

Stencil Making:

- Use holly wreath design from Father Christmas Quilt on page 48.
- Trace red bow and top of holly leaves.
- Trace holly leaves.
- Cut stencils, use paper punch for berries.

Stencil Painting:

- Mark placement of stencils (see photo of quilt).
- Do not paint until placement is correct.
- Holly leaf stencil must be reversed, flipped over for alternating design.
- Stencil must be cleaned each time it is used.
- Paint stencils in rows, alternating colors.
- Leaves and berries painted solid, pouncing method.
- Red bows should be shaded from light to dark, use streaking method. (Study quilt photo.)
- Heat set paint.

Assembling and Finishing:

- Layer quilt, baste and quilt. (See photo critique.)
- Trim edges.
- Bring green border to back of quilt and hem.

Right Photo:
Close-up shows quilting around the roses and ovals and the tufting within the block.

Left Photo:
Quilting details around roses and ovals are shown on the reverse side of the quilt.

Green Poinsettias

37" x 49" whole-cloth quilt with stenciled design, pictured on page 21.
(Intermediate)

Materials:

Quilt top:	½ white twin size sheet (take out hems)
Backing:	½ white twin size sheet (take out hems)
Batting:	1 crib size
Binding:	6 yds. bright red double fold commercial bias binding
Stencil:	1 - 12" x 12" plastic sheet
Acrylic Paint:	Bright green, bright red

Quilt Top Making:

- Mark 36" x 48" on whole-cloth, to be trimmed after quilting.
- Press center crease guidelines.

Stencil Making:

- Trace complete design on plastic sheet.
- Make red dot hole in corner of plastic sheet.

Stencil Painting:

- Mark complete stencil layout using crease guidelines.
- Refer to quilt photo.
- Paint in green with pouncing method.
- Use large stencil brush, up to 1".
- Paint red dots.
- Heat set paint.
- Mark quilting lines on white triangles. (See quilt photo.)

Assembling and Finishing:

- Layer quilt, baste and quilt. (See photo critique.)
- Trim edges.
- Add red bias binding and hem to quilt backing.

Green Poinsettias

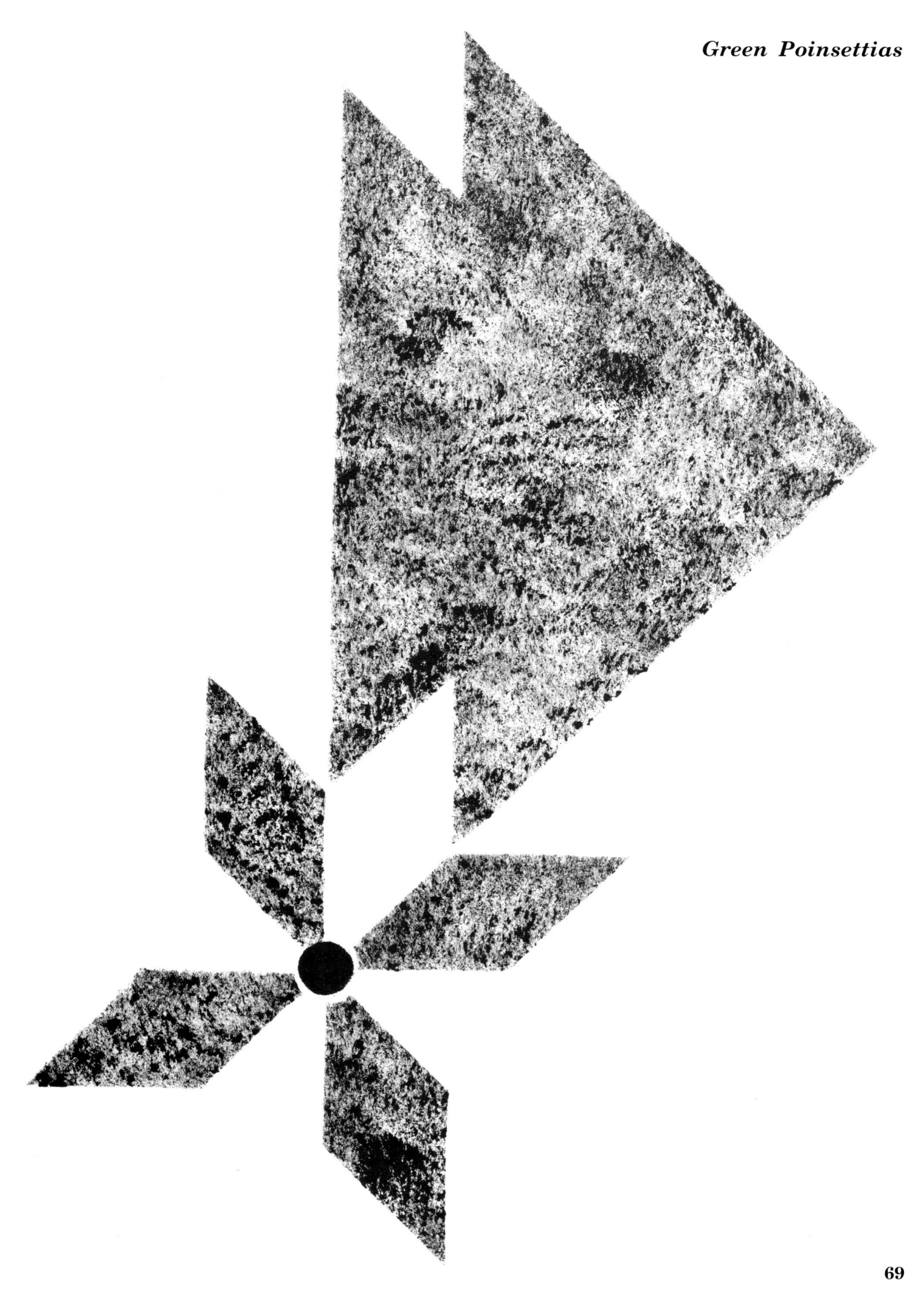

Hearts and Flowers

54" x 65½" patchwork quilt with stenciled design, pictured on page 22. (Intermediate)

Materials:

Quilt top:	2 yds. unbleached muslin
Sashing:	2 yds. dark green sashing and borders
	2 yds. red sashing and borders
Backing:	4 yds. unbleached muslin
Batting:	1 twin size
Stencil:	2 - 12" x 12" plastic sheets
Acrylic Paint:	Bright red, yellow-green, dark green

Quilt Top Making:

Cut 12 - 11½" x 11½" unbleached muslin blocks.
Cut 24 - 1½" x 11½" red sashing.
Cut 24 - 1½" x 13½" red sashing.
Cut 15 - 2" x 13½" green sashing.
Cut 6 - 2" x 60" green sashing.
Cut 4 - 1½" x 60" muslin sashing.
Cut 2 - 1½" x 52½" muslin sashing.
Cut 2 - 1½" x 52½" red border.
Cut 2 - 1½" x 63" red border.
Bind with 3" dark green sashing fabric.

- Stitch red sashing to blocks.
- Add green sashing on two sides making a row of four blocks, repeat two more times.
- Add long green sashing to each side of three block rows.
- Add muslin sashing.
- Add red border.

Stencil Making:

- See Glossary for stencil pattern note.
- Trace complete design on each sheet of plastic.
- Cut one stencil for red, the other for greens.

Stencil Painting:

- Paint red stencil first, then green stencils.
- Paint in solid, pouncing method.
- Heat set paint.

Assembling and Finishing:

- Layer quilt, baste and quilt. (See photo critique.)
- Trim edges.
- Add green binding, bring to backside of quilt and hem.

Hearts and Flowers

(See Glossary for Stencil Pattern Note)

The First Noel

24" x 31" whole-cloth quilt with stenciled design, pictured on page 23.

(Advanced)

Materials:

Quilt Top:	1¼" yd. tan whole-cloth and tan border
Borders:	¼ yd. green, ¼ yd. brown
Backing:	1¼" yd.
Batting:	28" x 36"
Stencil:	10 - 10" x 13" plastic sheets
Acrylic Paint:	Yellow ochre, dark green, dark brown, reddish brown, black

Quilt Top Making:

Cut 15" x 25" for whole-cloth tan fabric.
Cut 2 - 1½" x 17" green border.
Cut 2 - 1½" x 25" green border.
Cut 2 - 2" x 20" brown border.
Cut 2 - 2" x 27" brown border.
Cut 2 - 2" x 23" tan border.
Cut 2 - 2" x 30" tan border.
Cut 2 - 2½" x 27" brown outer border.
Cut 2 - 2½" x 33½" brown outer border.

- Add green border to whole-cloth.
- Add inner brown border.
- Add tan border.
- Add outer brown border.

Stencil Making:

- Trace complete 6 figure design on 5 sheets of plastic.
- Cut separate stencils for yellow ochre, dark brown, green, reddish brown, black.
- Trace complete 2 figure design on 5 sheets of plastic.
- Cut separate stencils for yellow ochre, dark brown, green, reddish brown, black.

Stencil Painting:

- Mark placement of stencils on whole-cloth fabric.
- Figures 2½" from bottom, 3" from sides.
- Paint colors starting with yellow ochre.
- Light brown in shepherds' robe is dark brown paint handled with a light touch.
- All other colors are painted in solid, pouncing method.
- Heat set paint.
- Mark quilting lines in background fabric. (See Glossary for Waffle quilting lines.)

Assembling and Finishing:

- Layer quilt, baste and quilt. (See photo critique.)
- Trim edges.
- Bring outer brown border to back of quilt and hem.

Quilting Line

Christmas Treats

45" x 51½" patchwork quilt with stenciled design, pictured on page 24.
(Intermediate)

Materials:

Quilt top:	½ white twin size sheet (take out hems)
Sashing:	2 yds. green and white polka dot fabric White sashing blocks from top fabric
Backing:	½ white twin size sheet (take out hems)
Batting:	Crib size
Stencil:	3 - 12" x 12" plastic sheets
Acrylic Paint:	Bright red, bright green, yellow ochre, dark brown

Quilt Top Making:

- Cut 12 - 9½" x 9½" white blocks.
  Cut 4 - 3" x 11¾" green (sashing corners).
  Cut 27 - 3" x 9½" green sashing.
  Cut 16 - 3" x 3" white sashing blocks.
  Cut 2 - 3" x 42½" white border.
  Cut 2 - 3" x 49" white border.
  Cut 2 - 3" x 54" green outer border.
  Cut 2 - 3" x 47½" green outer border.
- Add 5 sashing strips to 4 blocks, repeat 2 more times making 3 rows.
- Add 5 white sashing blocks to 4 green sashing strips, make 2 long sashing strips.
- Add sashing strip to 3 block rows.
- Make outer sashing strip using green corners and remaining 3" white sashing blocks.
- Add to outer blocks.
- Add white border.
- Add outer green border.

Stencil Making:

- Trace complete design on each plastic sheet.
- Cut one stencil for red, one for green and one for brown.
- Use paper punch for red dots.

Stencil Painting:

- Mark placement of circle design on each block.
- Paint circle design and green leaf stencil in solid, pouncing method.
- Paint brown basket stencil, paint yellow ochre first, shade in with dark brown.
- Paint red stencil in solid, pouncing method, shade berries a little with "dirty" dark brown brush.
- Heat set paint.
- Mark quilting X-lines on sashing and borders.

Assembling and Finishing:

- Layer quilt, baste and quilt. (See photo critique.)
- Trim edges.
- Bring outer green border to the quilt back and hem.

Quilting
Line

Laurel Rose

63½" x 84½" whole-cloth quilt with stenciled design, pictured on page 25.
(Advanced)

Materials:

Quilt top:	1 twin size white sheet (take out hems)
Backing:	1 twin size white sheet (take out hems)
Batting:	1 twin size
Binding:	9 yds. red double fold commercial bias binding
Stencil:	1 - 4" x 16" plastic sheet
	1 - 16" x 16" plastic sheet
Acrylic paint:	Bright red, dark bright green

Quilt Top Making:

- Mark 63" x 84" for whole-cloth to be trimmed after quilting.
- Press center crease guidelines.

Stencil Making:

- See Glossary for stencil pattern note.
- Trace complete Laurel Rose design on large plastic sheet.
- Cut green and red stencils from same sheet.
- Trace sawtooth border design on small plastic sheet, making a 13" repeat and cut.

Stencil Painting:

- Using pressed crease guidelines, center and mark all stencil designs for layout beginning in the center of the quilt top and working out to edge.
- All measuring and marks must be accurate.
- Center the red and green stencil in the middle of the quilt top, paint green then red before removing the stencil, repeat for all of center section of quilt top.
- Use a stenciling shield when painting red and green.
- Stencil paint sawtooth green border.
- Use ½ of large Laurel Rose design to paint outer border.
- Finish by painting outer sawtooth green border.
- Paint all colors in solid, pouncing method.
- Heat set paint.
- Make cardboard quilting template.
- Mark all football-shaped quilting lines around rose motif.

Assembling and Finishing:

- Layer quilt, baste and quilt. (See photo critique.)
- Trim edges.
- Add red bias binding and bring to back of quilt and hem.

Laurel Rose

(See Glossary for Stencil Pattern Note)

Laurel Rose

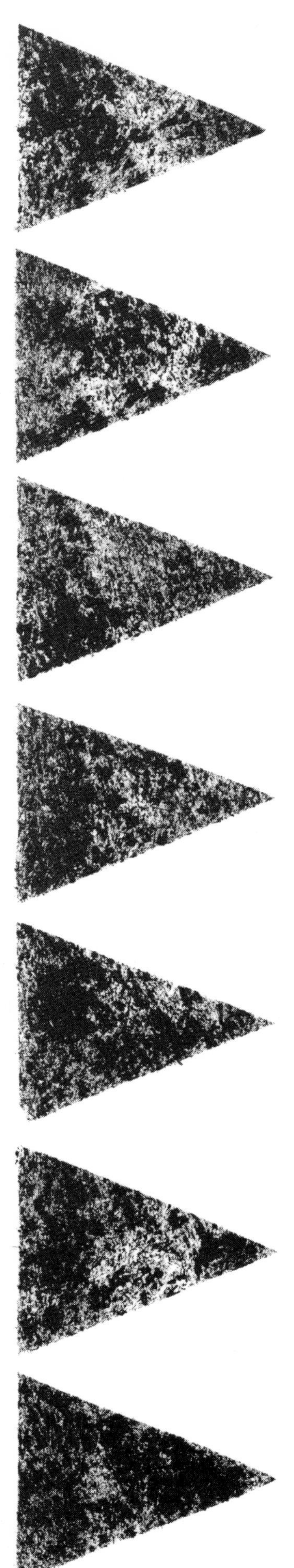

Quilting Line

Cardinals In A Pear Tree

30½" x 30½" patchwork quilt with stenciled design, pictured on page 26.
(Beginner)

Materials:

Quilt top:	1 yd. unbleached muslin
Sashing:	1 yd. bright red fabric
Backing:	1 yd. unbleached muslin
Batting:	1 sq. yd.
Stencil:	2 - 10" x 10" plastic sheets
Acrylic Paint:	Dark green, bright red, black, yellow ochre

Quilt Top Making:

- Cut 5 - 9½" x 9½" muslin blocks.
  Cut 4 - 9" x 9" x 12½" triangular muslin blocks.
  Cut 4 - 6½" x 6½" x 8½" triangular muslin corner blocks.
  Cut 10 - 1½" x 9½" red sashing.
  Cut 2 - 1½" x 31" red sashing.
  Cut 2 - 1½" x 27½" red border.
  Cut 2 - 1½ x 29" red border.
  Cut 2 - 2½" x 33½" muslin outer border.
  Cut 2 - 2½" x 29" muslin outer border.
- Add red sashing to blocks and triangles of muslin fabric.
- Join blocks. (See quilt photo.)
- Add red border.
- Add outer muslin border.

Stencil Making:

- Trace complete tree and bird design on each plastic sheet.
- Cut green stencil from one sheet; red birds and pear from other sheet.
- Cut black stencil for bird face. Use small leather punch for eye, place in corner of stencil sheet.

Stencil Painting:

- Center green stencil and paint.
- Paint red birds.
- Paint accents, face and pear.
- Paint in solid, pouncing method.
- Heat set paint.
- Mark parallel quilting lines on outer triangles.

Assembling and Finishing:

- Layer quilt, baste and quilt. (See photo critique.)
- Bring outer muslin border to back of quilt and hem.

Cardinals In A Pear Tree

Santas Big And Little

45" x 62½" patchwork quilt with stenciled design, pictured on page 27.
(Intermediate)

Materials:

Quilt top:	2 yds. bright green fabric
Sashing:	2 yds. bright red plaid fabric
Backing:	3 yds. green fabric
Batting:	1 twin size
Stencil:	9 - 8" x 10" plastic sheets
Acrylic Paint:	Bright red, black, white
Accent:	Red and black quilting thread

Quilt Top Making:

- Cut 15 - 8½" x 6" green blocks.
  Cut 2 - 8½" x 37½" green blocks.
  Cut 12 - 3" square green border blocks.
- Cut all sashing strips the same from the heart of the plaid.
  Cut 22 - 3" x 8½" plaid sashing.
  Cut 6 - 3" x 37½" plaid sashing.
  Cut 2 - 3" x 43" green outer border.
  Cut 2 - 3" x 60½" green outer border.
- Add 4 short sashing strips to 5 - 6" x 8½" green blocks, repeat making 3 rows of blocks.
- Add 5 short sashing strips to 6 green square blocks, repeat making 2 long pieced sashing strips.

Assembling Quilt Top:

- 6 long sashing strips alternating with row of green blocks and long single green block. (See quilt photo.)
- Add long pieced sashing to assembled blocks matching plaid and green corners.

Stencil Making:

- Plan for 3 stencils for each of 3 Santas.
- Trace complete Santa design on each plastic sheet.
- Cut for each Santa a red, black and white stencil.
- On a 2" plastic square, use leather punch for small eyes and nose.
- Same face for all Santas.
- Same stencil used for 5 Santas in a row.

Stencil Painting:

- Mark a line for bottom of feet to stand on.
- Mark center placement of Santas on blocks.
- Paint red first, white second, black last.
- Add face dots.
- Paint in solid, pouncing method.
- Heat set paint.

Assembling and Finishing:

- Layer quilt, baste and quilt. (See photo critique.)
- Trim edges.
- Turn outer green border to back of quilt and hem.

Holly Wreath

62½" x 75" patchwork quilt with stenciled design, pictured on 28.
(Intermediate)

Materials:

Quilt top:	2 yds. unbleached muslin
Sashing:	2 yds. bright red
	2 yds. dark green
Backing:	4 yds. unbleached muslin
Batting:	1 twin size
Stencil:	1 - 13" x 13" plastic sheet
Acrylic Paint:	Bright red, dark green, yellow green

Quilt Top Making:

- Cut 12 - 12" x 12" blocks.
  Cut 24 - 1½" x 12" red sashing.
  Cut 24 - 1½" x 14" red sashing.
  Cut 24 - 2" x 14" green sashing.
  Cut 9 - 1½" x 14" muslin spacers.
  Cut 6 - 2" x 69½" green sashing.
  Cut 4 - 1½" x 69½" red sashing (2 borders).
  Cut 2 - 1½" x 54" red border.
  Cut 2 - 2" x 71½" outer green border.
  Cut 2 - 2" x 57" outer green border.
- Add red sashing to frame each muslin block.
- Add 8 short green sashing strips to 4 red framed muslin blocks.
- Add 3 muslin spacers to 4 muslin framed blocks, to make a row.
- Repeat to make 3 rows of blocks.
- Add 2 long green sashing strips to either side of 3 block rows.
- Add 4 long red sashing strips to join 3 block rows.
- Add red sashing strip to top and bottom.
- Add outer green border.

Stencil Making:

- See Glossary for grid enlargement.
- Trace complete wreath design on single plastic sheet.
- Cut green leaf stencil and paper punch red dots.

Stencil Painting:

- Mask out red dot holes.
- Center stencil on quilt block and paint light green on half of leaf stencil.
- Finish painting leaf with dark green.
- Remove tape from red dots and mask out adjacent green leaves.
- Paint red dots.
- Heat set paint.
- Mark a 4½" inner quilting circle for wreath.
- Mark a 10½" outer quilting circle for wreath.

Assembling and Finishing:

- Layer quilt, baste and quilt. (See photo critique.)
- Trim edges.
- Bring quilt backing to the front and hem making a 1" border.

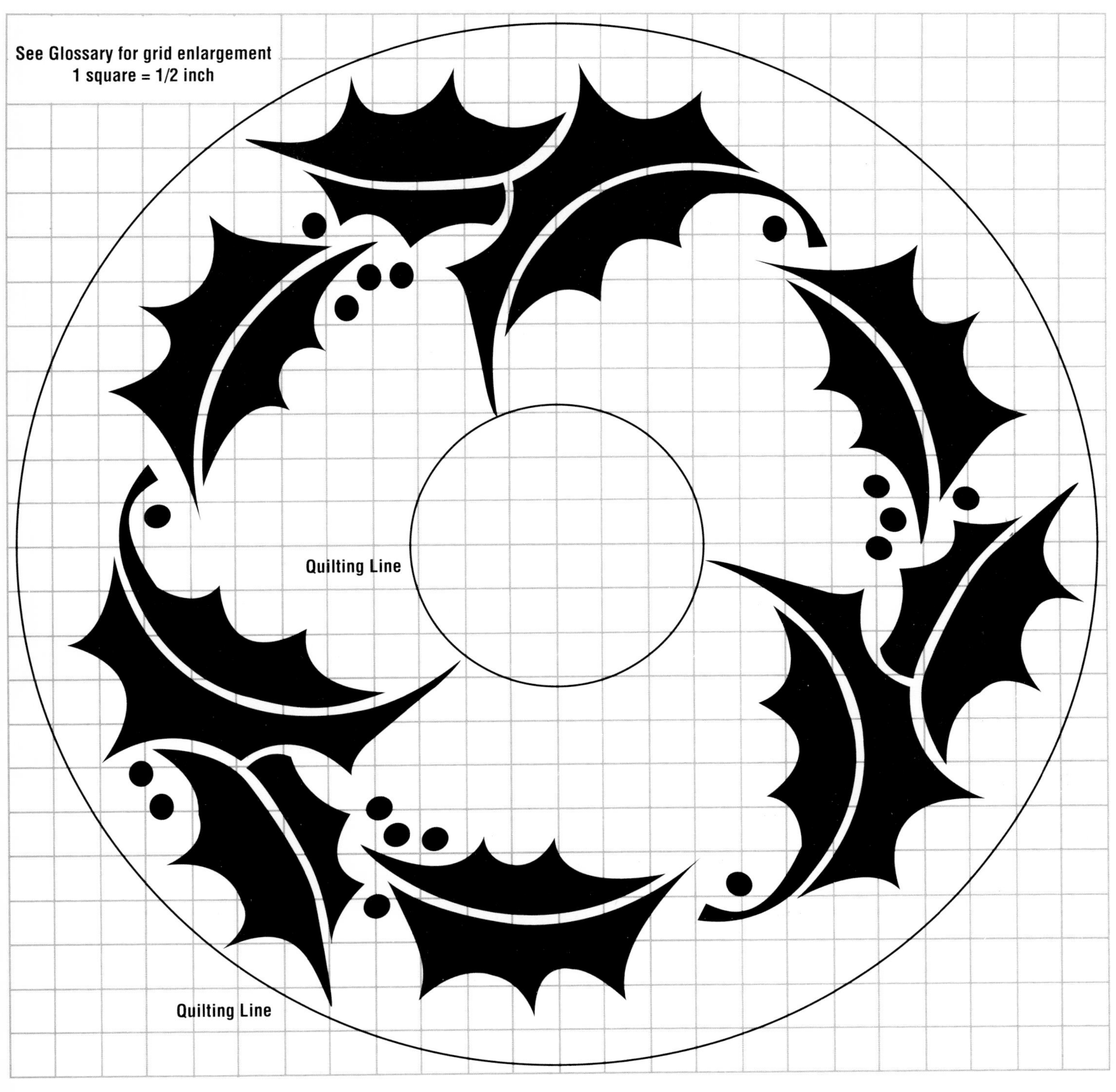
See Glossary for grid enlargement
1 square = 1/2 inch
Quilting Line
Quilting Line

Scarlet Ribbons

46½" x 57½" patchwork quilt with stenciled design, pictured on page 29. (Beginner)

Materials:

Quilt top:	½ white twin size sheet (take out hems)
Sashing:	2 yds. light green fabric
Backing:	½ white twin size sheet
Batting:	½ twin size
Binding:	6 yds. bright green double fold commerical bias binding
Stencil:	2 - 14" x 14" plastic sheets
Acrylic Paint:	Bright red, dark green

Quilt Top Making:

- Cut 12 - 11½" x 11½" white blocks.
  Cut 15 - 2" x 11½" green sashing.
  Cut 4 - 2" x 52" green sashing.
  Cut 2 - 3" x 39½" white border.
  Cut 2 - 3" x 57" white border.
  Cut 2 - 2½" x 57" outer green border.
  Cut 2 - 2½" x 48½" outer green border.
- Add 5 short green sashing strips to 4 white blocks, repeat to form 3 rows.
- Add 4 long green sashing strips to 3 rows of blocks.
- Add white border.
- Add outer green border.

Stencil Making:

- See Glossary for stencil pattern note.
- Trace complete stencil design on each plastic sheet.
- Cut a stencil for red. Use paper punch for dots.
- Cut a stencil for green.

Stencil Painting:

- Center red stencil on block and paint.
- Paint green stencil.
- Paint in solid, pouncing method.
- Heat set paint.
- Mark quilting lines on center of sashing strips.
- Mark a 4½" diagonal line across corners of white blocks.
- Mark 3" x 3" x 4½" diamonds on white border.

Assembling and Finishing:

- Layer quilt, baste and quilt. (See photo critique.)
- Trim edges.
- Add green bias binding and bring to the quilt back and hem.

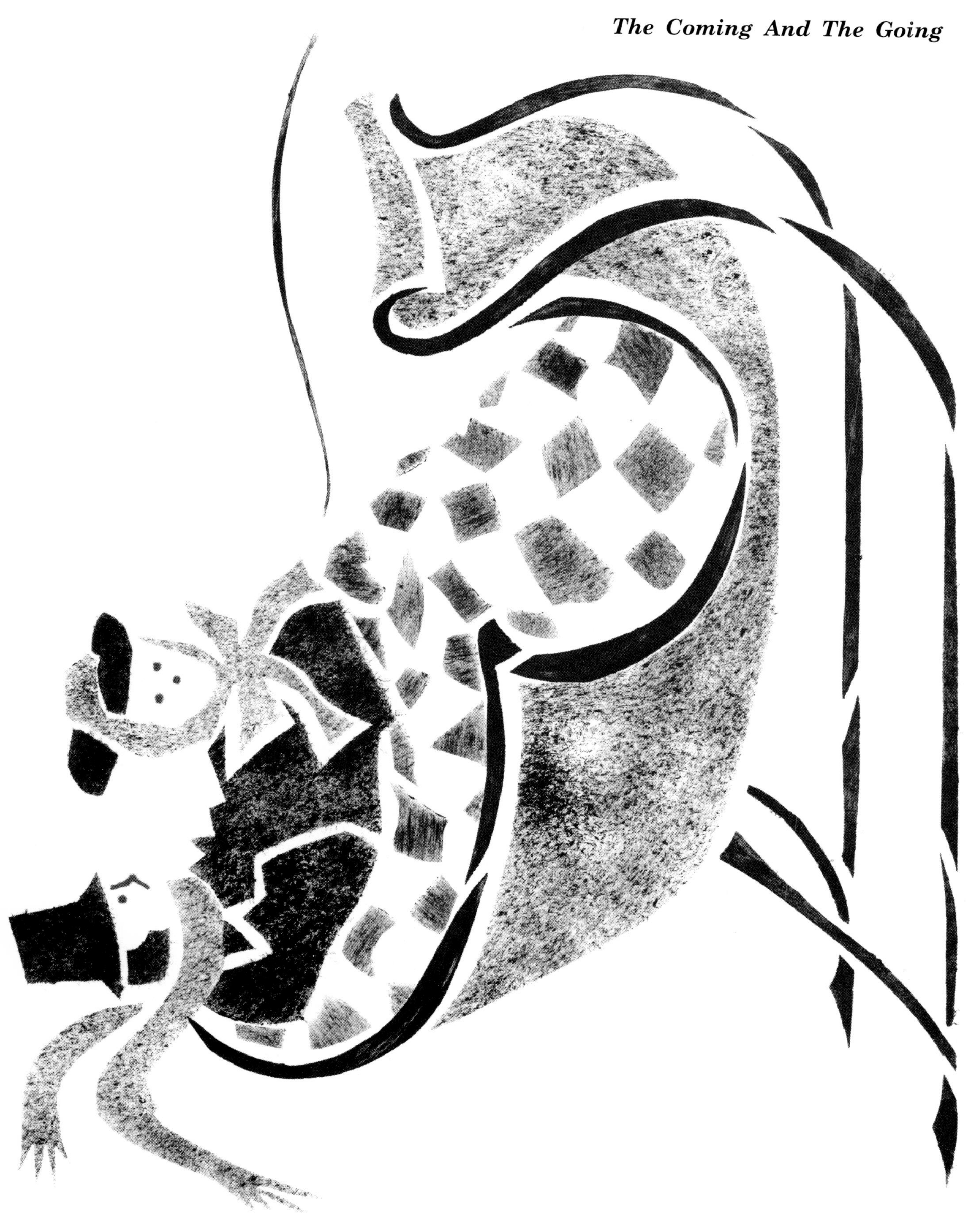

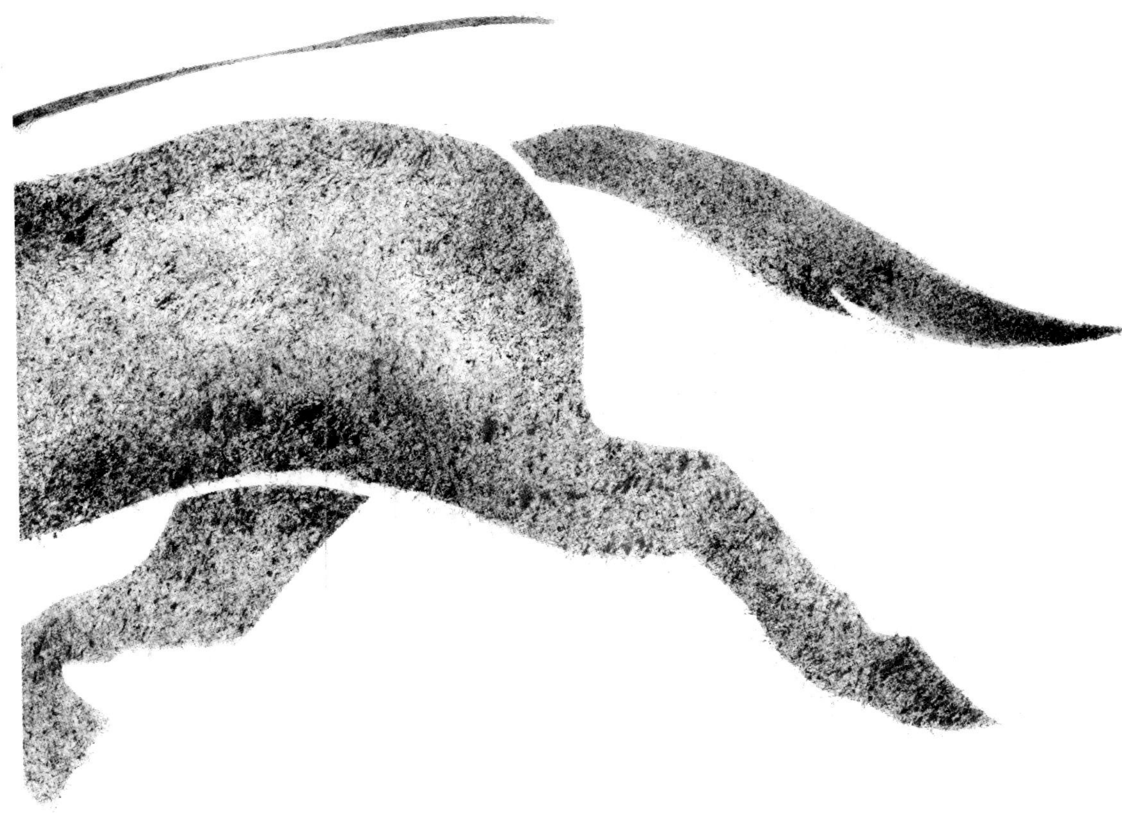

Loving Hearts

43½" x 58" patchwork quilt with stenciled design, pictured on page 31.
(Intermediate)

Materials:

Quilt top:	2 yds. unbleached muslin
Sashing:	1½ yd. dark green fabric
	1½ yd. bright red fabric
Backing:	2 yds. unbleached muslin
Batting:	1 crib size
Stencil:	2 - 10" x 10" plastic sheets
Acrylic Paint:	Bright red, dark green

Quilt Top Making:

- Cut 12 - 10" x 10" muslin blocks.
  Cut 15 - 2" x 10" green sashing.
  Cut 4 - 2" x 46" green sashing.
  Cut 2 - 1½" x 48" red border.
  Cut 2 - 1½" x 35" red border.
  Cut 2 - 3" x 37" muslin border.
  Cut 2 - 3" x 53" muslin border.
  Cut 2 - 2" x 56" outer green border.
  Cut 2 - 2" x 42" outer green border.
- Add 5 short green sashing strips to 4 muslin blocks.
- Repeat to make 3 rows of muslin blocks.
- Add 4 long green sashing strips to 3 rows of muslin blocks.
- Add red border.
- Add muslin border.
- Add outer green border.

Stencil Making:

- Trace complete stencil design on each plastic sheet.
- Cut one stencil for red; another for green.

Stencil Painting:

- Center red stencil on muslin block and paint.
- Paint green stencil.
- Paint in solid, pouncing method.
- Heat set paint.

Assembling and Finishing:

- Layer quilt, baste and quilt. (See photo critique.)
- Trim edges.
- Bring muslin quilt backing to the top of the quilt and hem.

Bright Star

45" x 61½" whole-cloth quilt with stenciled design, pictured on page 32.
(Intermediate)

Materials:

Quilt top: 44" x 60½" whole-cloth unbleached muslin
Backing: 2 yds. 54" unbleached muslin
Batting: 1 twin size
Binding: 6 yds. red double fold commercial bias binding
Stencil: 2 - 12" x 12" plastic sheets
Acrylic Paint: Bright red, bright blue

Quilt Top Making:

- Mark 45" x 61½" on whole-cloth, to be trimmed after quilting.
- Press center crease lines in whole-cloth.

Stencil Making:

- Trace complete design on each plastic sheet.
- Cut one stencil for red; the other for blue.

Stencil Painting:

- Mark placements of stencil on whole-cloth.
- Make use of crease guidelines.
- Paint blue stars first.
- Use 1" stencil brush with streaking movement.
- Do not paint the center part of the blue star.
- Paint red star on top of blue star.
- Paint red in solid pouncing method.
- Heat set paint.
- Make cardboard quilting template for large hexagons from stencil pattern.
- Mark quilting lines.

Assembling and Finishing:

- Layer quilt, baste and quilt. (See photo critique.)
- Trim edges.
- Add red bias binding and hem to the back side.

Bright Star

Glossary

Acrylic: A water base paint that dries to a permanent state. Purchased as an artist paint in tubes or as an interior or exterior house paint. All three are acceptable for stencil painting on fabric. Must be heat set. Soap and water clean up.

Applique: Fabric cut to a design and hand or machine stitched to a fabric background. Hand applique stitches are:

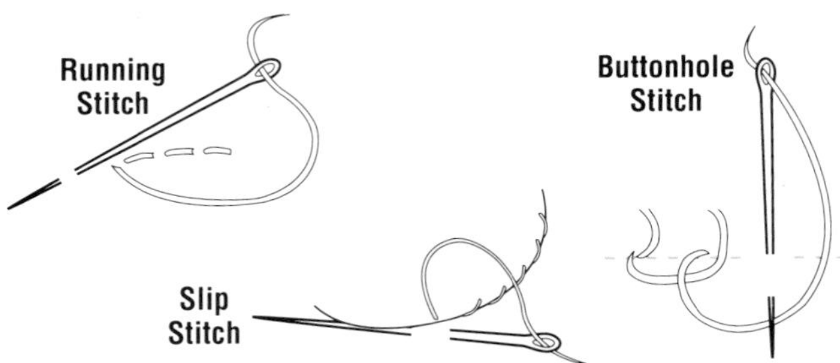

Backing: Fabric comprising the bottom side of a quilt and is usually made of two large pieces of fabric because of its size. Print or solid-color fabric can be used.

Back Stitch: Taking a single stitch behind the thread where it comes up out of the fabric. A good locking stitch to end off a thread.

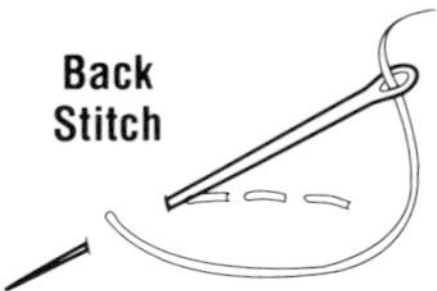

Basting Stitch: Usually made with a large eye needle 2¼" long which makes a stitch about 2" long, used to hold the three layers of the quilt together for the quilting process. Use a back stitch to begin and end a row of basting stitches.

Batting: Cotton, wool or polyester fiber sheet sandwiched between the quilt top and the quilt backing. Polyester batting comes in several thicknesses (lofts) and five sizes - crib (45" x 60"), twin (72" x 90"), full (81" x 96"), queen (90" x 108") and king (120" x 120"). Thin batting will help to produce short even stitches; thick batting will not. Unfold and allow batting to relax overnight to remove creases.

Bias: Fabric strips cut on a diagonal line of the fabric. A 45° angle cut from the straight grain of the fabric.

Binding: Fabric strips about three inches wide cut on the bias or straight of the fabric and used to finish the raw edges of quilt. Double fold commercial bias can be purchased in many colors.

Block: A patch or patches of fabric of various sizes assembled to make a unit. Many block units may comprise a quilt top.

Borders: Vertical and horizontal strips of fabric that create a picture frame effect, containing the center of the quilt. If several borders are used, the inner borders are usually narrow, the outer borders wide.

Brushes: Stencil brushes are round and have short stiff bristles and come in six sizes. No. 4 (⅜"), No. 8 (½"), and 1" brushes are the most common sizes. Most any stiff round brush can be used for stenciling if masking tape is wrapped around the bristles exposing just ½" of the bristles. The end of the brush should be flat.

Comforter: A bed covering with a batting too thick to be successfully quilted, and is tied or tufted with wool yarn to secure the quilt top, batting and backing.

Grain: The direction of the threads in the fabric. Lengthwise is the warp; crosswise is the woof.

Grid Pattern Enlargement: Stencil patterns that are larger than the page are drawn on a grid plan and must be enlarged. Any design presented on a grid can be enlarged on a copy machine. The larger designs copied on several sheets can be taped together to complete the full design. Each grid square enlarges to equal a ½" square. On your grid paper draw ½" squares to equal the number on the grid plan. Working square by square, draw the lines as they appear in each square of the grid plan. Your plan paper now can be used for tracing the stencil design onto plastic sheets.

Hand Quilting: A running stitch worked through the three layers of a quilt to hold it together. Stitches worked in a fancy design such as plumes, feathers or shells can give the quilt a decorative dimension.

Heat Set: Acrylic or latex paint must be treated with heat to make it more permanent. Iron the dry stencil painted areas with a hot iron on the back side first. This draws the paint into the fabric. Iron on the painted top using a pressing cloth.

Iron and Ironing Board: Sometimes quiltmaking is made much easier with a steam iron. Use the small end of the ironing board for the iron rest, allowing more width to press large pieces of fabric.

Latex: A water base paint that is similar in performance to acrylic paint.

Lattice Strips: Interchangeable term with sashing strips, mullion strips.

Medallion Quilt: A quilt top that has one large design usually framed with several borders and can be set on its point or squared with the outer edges of the quilt. Ovals or circles can also be used for the dominate center design.

Markers: Water soluble marking pens are invaluable for quiltmaking. Test first to determine if the color will rinse out of the fabric with water. Some markers are fast fading.

Mitered Corners: Two pieces of fabric joined at right angles forming a 45° seam. Borders and sashing look nice with mitered corners. A simpler way to finish a corner is the butted method.

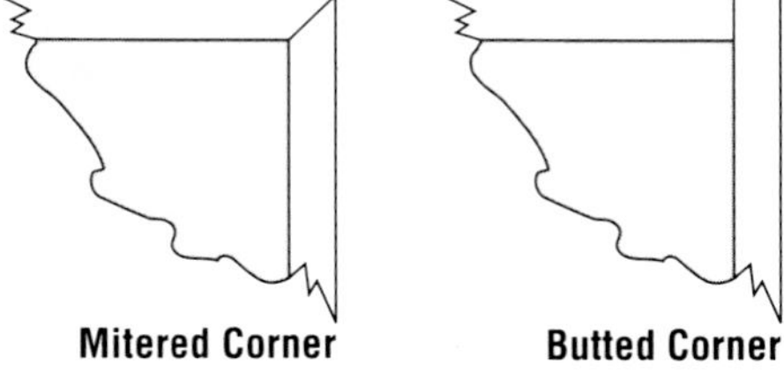

Mylar ™ : A brand name for a durable frosted plastic used for stencil making. Comes in sheets 2' x 3', available at engineering/drafting supply companies or in smaller sheets at craft stores.

Needles: Quilting needles are called "Betweens," popular sizes are 7 through 10. The larger the number the shorter the needles. "Sharp" needles, made of thinner metal are good for hand sewing.

Palette: A plastic butter carton lid makes a good container for holding stencil paint.

Patchwork: Pieces of fabric in numerous sizes and colors stitched together to form a quilt top, sometimes incorporating applique methods and stencil painting.

Pieced: A single shape of fabric joined with other shapes to create a pieced design. Pieces are also said to be patched together.

Pins: Special straight plastic headed pins 1¾" long are ideal for quiltmaking.

Quilting Frames: Traditional frames consist of 2 long rails and 2 short rails clamped together at the corners in a rectangular position. The quilt top, batting and backing are secured to two of the rails by heavy basting threads and rolled onto the rails, stretching the quilt taut in readiness for quilting.

Quilting Hoop: Circular or oval wood shapes for holding the quilt in place during the quilting process. Popular sizes: round 14" and 18", oval 16" x 27". Stands 31" high are available. Lap frames that handle much like a hoop are adjustable from a 4" square to a 22" square.

Quilting In The Ditch: Working the quilting stitches very close to a stitched seam.

Quilter's Masking Tape: Comes in widths of ⅛", ¼", ½" and ¾" and is used to guide the stitching of quilting lines.

Quilt Top: There are basically two different types of quilt tops - patchwork and whole-cloth.

Rotary Cutter: Shaped much like a pizza cutter and produces precision cuts of fabric. The cutter requires a special cutting base (good size - 8" and 24") and is most effectively used with a 6" x 24" gridded transparent ruler.

Sashing: Individual frames of fabric surrounding a quilt block ranging in width from 1" to 4". They resemble the cut-ups or mullion bars of a colonial-type window. Lattice, sashing and mullion are all interchangeable terms.

Set: A systematic way of assembling quilt blocks, sashing and borders to form a quilt top.

Shellac Thinner: Used for cleaning dried acrylic or latex paint from plastic stencils.

Stencil Pattern Note: All stencil patterns given in this book that do not show the full design can be completed by revolving the pencil copied part of the design to overlap a corresponding part of the printed stencil pattern.

Stenciling Props: Pieces of open patterned

materials that can be stenciled over to create a painted textured design. Examples: chicken wire, hardware cloth, window screen, and plastic onion bags.

Stenciling Shield: A scrap piece of plastic used to safeguard against smudging paint in unwanted areas.

Template: A pattern for marking a fabric shape or for marking a line design for quilting. It can be made of plastic or heavy cardboard. A stencil can be used as a template for marking quilting lines.

Thimble: Quilting thimbles come in all sizes and shapes and made from leather, plastic or metal. The important thing is you will never become a good quilter without the use of a thimble.

Thread: The best quilting threads are made of cotton. An extra strong hand quilting thread that is cotton covered polyester is very satisfactory. Quilting thread comes in a variety of colors. Thread cut on a slant is easier to pass through the eye of a needle.

Tied or Tufted: The layers of the quilt are held together by tying strands of yarn or heavy embroidery floss not more than six inches apart. To thread yarn, hold needle by the eye end, loop yarn over point end of needle, pull yarn tight and remove the needle. With the taut yarn between pinched thumb and first finger, place needle eye over yarn and pull the yarn through the eye. #3 darner's needle works well. Wool yarn does not slip when tied in a square knot.

Waffle quilting lines: Place a dot, with water-color fabric marker, at the center edge of the fabric on all four sides. Place the edge of the yardstick on top dot and right side dot; draw a line on either side of the yardstick. Repeat for left hand side. Space between lines will be the width of the stick or usually 1¼" wide. To create the diamond shapes, move the yardstick even with the last line and continue marking one line at a time. Another way is to draw diagonal crisscross lines from corner to corner and repeat the use of parallel lines.

Whole-cloth: A single large cloth often made from several widths of fabric stitched together. Whole-cloth quilts can be stencil painted and quilted, just quilted with an overall design called "white work" or appliqued and quilted.

Your Quilt Care: Wash only if necessary. Add a mild detergent to empty washer and fill with tepid water. Place quilt in washer and hand agitate to wet all fabric. Allow to soak five minutes. Gently squeeze to determine if quilt is clean. Set washer on spin cycle to remove soapy water. Refill washer with rinse water, hand agitate and spin dry. Repeat if necessary. The centrifugal force of the spin cycle will not damage the quilt. Remove quilt from washer and dry flat on a bed. Do not ever use chlorine bleach on a stenciled quilt nor dry clean. Store quilts in cloth bags, never in plastic bags nor where they might touch raw wood. To display a quilt, sew a 4" wide cloth casing across the top of the quilt, insert a dowel rod and hang with transparent fishing line.

Bibliography

Bacon, Lenice Ingram
American Patchwork Quilts
New York: Bonanza Books, 1980

Better Homes and Gardens, eds.
Better Homes and Gardens American Patchwork and Quilting
Des Moines, IA: Meredith Corp., 1985

Bishop, Adele and Cile Lord
The Art of Decorative Stenciling, rev. ed.
New York: Penguin Books, Inc., 1985

Bonesteel, Georga
New Ideas for Lap Quilting
Birmingham, AL: Oxmoor House, Inc., 1987

Fjelstul, Schad, and Barbara Marhoefer
More Early American Stencils in Color
New York: E.P. Dutton Co., 1986

Hassel, Carla J.
Super Quilter II
Des Moines: Wallace-Homestead, 1982

Hopf, Claudia
Scherenschnitte For All Seasons
Kennebunk, ME, Hopf Publications, 1986

Houch, Carter and Myran Miller
American Quilts and How to Make Them
New York: Charles Scribner's Son, 1975

Jones, Owen
The Grammar of Ornament
New York, Dover Publications, Inc., 1987

LeGrice, Lyn
The Art of Stenciling
New York: Crown Publishing, Inc., 1986

MacDowell, Marsha and Ruth D. Fitzgerald
Michigan Quilts, 150 Years of a Textile Tradition
East Lansing, Michigan, Michigan State University Museum, 1987.

Marston, Gwen and Joe Cunningham
Sets and Borders
Paducah, KY: American Quilters' Society, 1987

Martin, Nancy J.
Pieces of the Past
Bothell, WA: The Patchwork Place, Inc. 1986

McCall's, eds.
McCall's Big Book of Needlecrafts
Radnor, PA: Chilton Books Co., 1982

McKim, Ruby S.
101 Patchwork Patterns, rev. ed.
New York: Dover Publishing, Inc., 1962

O'Brien, Sandra L.
Great American Quilts 1987
Great American Quilts 1988
Birmingham, AL, Oxmoor House, Inc. 1987-1988

Safford, Carleton L., and Robert Bishop
America's Quilts and Coverlets
New York: Doer Publishing, Inc., 1937

Sturmer, Marie
The Stenciled Quilt
Dublin, NH: Yankee Books, 1986

Waring, Janet
Early American Stencils on Walls and Furniture
New York: Dover Publishing, Inc., 1937

Woodard, Thomas and Blanche Greenstein
Crib Quilts and other Small Wonders
New York: Bonanza Books, 1988

Stencil Suppliers

Adele Bishop, Inc.
P.O. Box 3349
Kinston, NC 28502-3349
(Fabric paints and Japan paints)

Avery-Morgan Ltd.
New England Stencil Co.
P.O. Box 253
Old Mystic, CT 06372
(Fab-Tex water-based paints)

Eastern Craft Supply
P.O. Box 341, Dept. 6800
Wyckoff, NJ 07481
(Fabric acrylic paint kits)

Gail Grisi Stenciling, Inc.
P.O. Box 1263
Haddonfield, NJ 08033
(Historic Philadelphia acrylic paints)

Plaid Enterprises, Inc.
P.O. Box 7600
Norcross, GA 30091
(Stencil Decor paints)

Sten Art, Inc.
P.O. Box 114
Pitman, NJ 08071-0114
(Kits and precut stencils)

Stencil-Ease
P.O. Box 282
14 Powder Hill Dr.
Lincoln, RI 02865
(Fab-Tex and Japan paints)

Stencilers Emporium
86 Owen-Brown St.
P.O. Box 6039
Hudson, OH 44236-6039
(Membership required)

Stencil House
RFD 9, Box 287
Concord, NH 03301
(Shiva oil-based Paintstiks)

Stencil School
P.O. Box 94
Shrewsbury, MA 01545
(Precut stencils)